Your Relationship with God

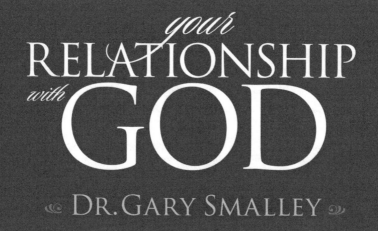

your
RELATIONSHIP
with GOD

DR. GARY SMALLEY

TYNDALE HOUSE PUBLISHERS, INC., CAROL STREAM, ILLINOIS

Visit Tyndale's exciting Web site at www.tyndale.com

TYNDALE and Tyndale's quill logo are registered trademarks of Tyndale House Publishers, Inc.

Your Relationship with God

Copyright © 2006 by Smalley Publishing Group LLC. All rights reserved.

Cover photo of grass copyright © by Harrison Smith/Alamy. All rights reserved.

Cover photo of ocean copyright © by Veer. All rights reserved.

Author photo copyright © by Jim Lersch. All rights reserved.

Designed by Jennifer Ghionzoli

Edited by Dave Lindstedt

Published in association with the literary agency of Alive Communications, Inc., 7680 Goddard Street, Suite 200, Colorado Springs, CO 80920.

Library of Congress Cataloging-in-Publication Data

Smalley, Gary.
    Your relationship with God / Gary Smalley.
        p. cm.
    Includes bibliographical references.
    ISBN-13: 978-0-8423-8323-3 (hc)
    ISBN-10: 0-8423-8323-9 (hc)
    ISBN-13: 978-1-4143-0446-5 (sc)
    ISBN-10: 1-4143-0446-3 (sc)
    1. Spirituality.   I. Title.
BV4501.3.S63 2006
248.4—dc22   2006016772

Printed in the United States of America

13   12   11   10   09   08   07
 7   6   5   4   3   2   1

DEDICATION

I enthusiastically dedicate this book to my younger son,
Michael Thomas Smalley.
Michael constantly gives me encouragement, joy, and inspiration.
Even more amazing, he gave me part of himself—
one of his kidneys—
to keep me alive and ministering,
so that we can both continue loving God and others.

CONTENTS

ACKNOWLEDGMENTS

I thank God that my relationship with him has not only been restored but has reached a level I have never before experienced. He is more than worthy of my praise!

A giant thanks goes to my writing team: Terry Brown, Ted Cunningham, and Sue Parks. This project was a joy to do as a team. And to my wife, Norma, my biggest support during all my speaking engagements, book projects, and trials. She is a gift from God. Special thanks to writer Tracey Lawrence, who helped me develop the original draft of this book. Thank you also to the entire Tyndale team, including our project leader, Jon Farrar; editor and great servant Dave Lindstedt; designer Jennifer Ghionzoli; marketing manager Maria Eriksen; and copy editor Joan Hutcheson.

REALITY CHECK

MAKING A MESS
OF SUCCESS

"What is *taking* so long?" I fumed as I waited for the doctors to arrive to begin my kidney transplant operation. I was lying on a bed in a pre-op room, wearing one of those wonderful hospital gowns—you know the type. The room was fairly cold and the nurses were bustling about doing what nurses do, not paying much attention to me. I was in sort of a twilight zone, but it seemed as if I had been cooling my heels for hours—and patience had never been one of my strengths. All I knew was that I was cold, uncomfortable, and apprehensive about the transplant and that I wanted to get it over with.

What I didn't know was that at that very moment, in the room next door, my son Michael was fighting for his life. As the doctors removed the kidney that Michael was donating to me, one of his lungs collapsed and his situation became perilous. While they were working to stabilize my son's condition, I was grumping and grousing in the next room about the inconvenience of having to wait.

I open with this story because in a lot of ways it sums up a major crisis in my life that had encompassed my physical, emotional, and spiritual health for years. I hadn't intended to end up self-absorbed, physically sick, emotionally out of balance, and spiritually isolated, but that's what happened. I was angry, impatient, disappointed, and frustrated with a lot of things in my life—and I was under a *ton* of stress. Along the way I had stopped relying on God and began to lean heavily on my own understanding and my own resources. The results were a major spiritual and emotional burnout and some very serious physical problems.

I want to share my story with you because I've found that most people, in one way or another and at one time or another, find themselves in similar circumstances: fed up, burned out, frustrated, and out of step with God. Maybe you are going through a similar struggle in your own life right now. Perhaps you, too, have experienced the joy that comes from a relationship with Jesus Christ. Then, through the busyness of life, being pulled in every direction, you've lost your bearings and drifted away from God's best plan for you.

If the truth be told, we're all susceptible to drifting. There are so many voices in our culture that compete with God's voice for our attention. We begin to believe that we need *more* to be happy. More power. More love. More sex. More food. More travel. More things. These voices grow louder and louder, and soon we ignore the voice in our spirit that cries out, "No! We don't need more *things;* we just need more of *God.*" As Jesus said, "What good is it for a man to gain the whole world, yet forfeit his soul?"[1]

It can happen suddenly, or gradually. If our guard is down, we can easily fall prey to the whims of the world. I know firsthand what it feels like to succumb to the temptation for more things, more money, more recognition, more comfort, and more leisure. Though I achieved just about everything I could possibly want in a material sense, I lost life's satisfaction and the enjoyment of God's blessings for a period of about ten years. I was miserable, and I wasn't sure if I could ever regain the joy I had once known.

Fortunately, that's not the end of the story, or I wouldn't be writing this book. I also want to tell you about a miraculous renewal that began during my recovery from the kidney transplant and that is still bearing fruit in my life to this day. I'm a new man, with a fresh perspective on life. In the process of this renewal, I learned some important principles that I believe will help you move toward renewal in your own life and in your relationship with God.

What follows is the story of how I lost sight of my relationship with God for a while and how I began to drift away from him—even though I knew better, even though I've been teaching about how to have successful relationships for almost my entire career. Happily, this is also the story of how I was suddenly awakened to renew my relationship with God.

If this were only my own story of wandering away from God, it might be of limited use or interest, but I have seen the same principles—both positive and negative—played out in the lives of so many of the people I have counseled over the years, people who have read my books and attended my seminars. My hope is that if you hear the inside story—and the *rest* of the story—it might inspire you to draw closer to God and to experience the same renewal, refreshment, and revitalization that I have experienced.

Looking back, I can see how easy it was for me to drift away from God. Perhaps you've drifted in a similar way. Life gets busy, and a lot of demands are placed on our time. We get focused on the details of everyday life and on becoming successful at what we do, whether it's raising a family, running a business, or working at a job. We might suffer some setbacks or get distracted, and before we know it, we've gotten out of the habit of spending regular time with

God and reading his Word. We just start doing things on our own, pursuing our own goals, and making decisions based on our own self-interest. We still go to church and give lip service to our relationship with God, but before long he starts to seem pretty distant.

I've counseled enough people over the past thirty years to know that getting off track is a common problem. Still, it's embarrassing to think about how far I actually wandered before God got my attention again. After all, I've been to seminary and served on a pastoral staff, and like a lot of other Christians, I've heard some of the best Bible teaching anyone could possibly hear. But even with all that, it didn't take much for me to become distracted from my relationship with God by all the cares and concerns of life. The success itself became a distraction. The process was so gradual that I couldn't see it for what it was—ugly, sinful, and destructive—until it was almost too late.

How I Got Off Track

When I began earnestly pursuing God's calling on my life back in the 1960s and 1970s, I never dreamed that I would eventually encounter such success. Although my career got off to a promising start, one of my first jobs, in a ministry organization, took a turn for the worse after several years and ended badly, leaving me feeling confused and discouraged. When I left that organization, Norma and I moved to Waco, Texas, where I became a family pastor in a church. In this new job and new surroundings, I felt that God was renewing my spirit and healing old wounds. It was like a breath of fresh air. I felt as if Christ once again became the center of my life. Not that everything was perfect in Waco—every situation has its challenges—but I felt renewed in my relationship with God, and he began to bless me and my work.

During those years, I remember setting aside time each day for prayer, and praying with such focus and intensity that I believed everything I prayed for would eventually come to pass in some way. My prayers were people centered, and I prayed with big results in mind. I was energized to reach thousands of people for Christ and help thousands of marriages. At least, that was my vision and I believed that God desired to use me in that way.

> I was energized to reach thousands of people for Christ and help thousands of marriages because I believed that God desired to use me in that way.

After I had been in Waco for about a year, I received a phone call from my good friend Steve Scott. Steve and his wife had attended one of my weekend marriage retreats, and he had come away with a new excitement about his marriage.

"Gary," he said, "you've got to write this stuff down. Have you ever thought about writing a book about marriage?"

I didn't know if I had what it takes to write a book—the writing process and my ADD don't always make great bedfellows—but I had been thinking about how I could expand my message to reach more people. I asked Steve if he would pray with me about it, and he agreed.

We began praying, and within six months we had a plan to write not just one book but two—one for men, and the other for women. Although I had no formal training in writing, Steve was a talented advertising writer. We worked together, and during that next year we finished the books.

In 1979, my church sent me out to be a "missionary to the world" to help couples, singles, and parents in their relationships. I taught seminars about twice a month. By the mid-1980s, Norma and I had moved to Phoenix; I had published several more books,

which were all selling well; and the seminar ministry was really taking off. We changed the name of our organization to Today's Family
and hired more staff to take our ministry nationwide.

In 1988, Steve Scott and I filmed an infomercial, hosted by
Dick Clark, to sell videotapes of my seminars. We later updated
these infomercials, with the help of John Tesh and Connie Sellecca,
and Frank and Kathie Lee Gifford. The video series sold more than
four million copies.

With the sale of all those tapes and a steady stream of book
royalties coming in, you can imagine how much money we now had
to handle. I know, it sounds like a great problem to have—and in
many ways it was—but it created some
pressure points, both in my life and in
my relationships, that would later
cause some serious fractures.

> Money began to create some pressure points, both in my life and in my relationships, that would later cause some serious fractures.

I grew up in a very poor family
and never had much money. Early in
my career, when I was an assistant pastor, I was earning just enough to provide from month to month for my wife
and three kids. And I was happy. I
would start my days with a morning jog, taking time to thank God
for all the blessings in my life. Life was good. I felt healthy and successful, and I was excited about my relationship with God. I specifically remember telling him that I didn't need money, that all I
wanted was to love people and minister to them.

But when the money started rolling in, I found I was ill-
prepared to handle it. I had never learned anything about saving,
investing, giving, or anything else related to business or personal
finances. I had always been the one trying to raise money for ministry; now other people were coming to me for financial help.

The amount of money that came into our ministry changed from month to month, and I didn't have a clue about how to manage it. But I wasn't worried. I believed that God was allowing our ministry to prosper and that he would guide us. I certainly wasn't worried about becoming corrupted.

I still remember sitting with my good friend Dave Cavan at his conference table and saying, "Dave, don't worry about me. My relationship with Christ is so close that money will not have the same effect on me that it might have had in the past." Well, I was wrong. Money did have a hold on me. The Bible warns us not to be naive in believing that we are above falling into temptation and sin. I was pretty naive.

Here I was, with more money than I'd ever seen and a ministry that was going off the charts in terms of growth. Even though my passion was with the ministry, not with making a lot of money, all of a sudden both the ministry and the money were begging for my attention, and God was only somewhere in the mix. I was becoming distracted from my primary relationship by the sheer volume and pace of life. Sound familiar?

As time went on, I began acquiring things—investment properties, new cars, snowmobiles, a boat. I told myself these things were all for my family's enjoyment, but being able to provide these nice things was just as much about satisfying my own ego. Just five years before, I had taught about the dangers of materialism and how rising expectations can cause stress and destroy relationships. Yet here I was, ignoring God's truth by doing the very things I had warned against.

> I believed that God was allowing our ministry to prosper and that he would guide us. I certainly wasn't worried about becoming corrupted.

I now understand more clearly why money doesn't bring more happiness. The more we have, the more it controls what we do. After a while, I stopped asking God, "Is this something you want me to have?" If I saw something I wanted, I just went ahead and bought it.

Sometimes, I didn't even tell Norma what I was planning to do. A classic example of this was the time I started construction on a new house without talking to Norma about it.

> I now understand more clearly why money doesn't bring more happiness. The more we have, the more it controls what we do.

It was several years ago that Norma and I decided to move closer to our present ministry office in Branson, Missouri. With our kids all grown and gone (though they were all living nearby at the time), we decided we could downsize our home and save some money. We had already purchased a lot through a close friend, so we had the land; all we needed was a plan. Norma mentioned to me that she really wanted to wait until we sold the house we were living in so we would not be stretched financially.

Even though I remembered Norma giving me that advice, I began to dream about a house design I had seen in Philadelphia. The house had lots of brick and kind of an English country feel to it. I figured it wouldn't hurt to meet with the builder and at least discuss preliminary plans. When we got together, he told me he had built a similar home in California and could save us a lot of money. Without consulting Norma, I told the builder, "Let's go ahead and get started, but let's keep it a secret."

I showed Norma the plans, and she agreed to the English look, the size, and the floor plan. What she didn't know was that the house was already under construction. When I met with our banker, he told me that all he needed to finish the paperwork was my wife's signature. I realized that I couldn't keep my surprise. I had to tell her.

I took Norma to lunch and told her I wanted to share some "good news" and some "not so good news." When she asked for the "not so good news" first, I told her I had met with the builder and that the house was already underway.

She got very silent. In Norma language that means, "You're in big trouble, pal." Taking advantage of the silence, I quickly added a little sales pitch: "But I talked with our real estate agent again, and she said we should have several offers for our home in the first three weeks of being on the market."

Norma finally signed the papers, but she let me know that she didn't appreciate my little surprise.

Three weeks later, Norma said to me, sort of in jest but sort of not, "Ah, Gary, you said we'd have several offers within the first three weeks and we haven't had one!" Once again, Norma was right.

Several months passed, and still no offers. By now it was time to move into our new home. Although moving into the new house was very exciting and fulfilling, the weight around our necks—two monthly mortgage payments—was exactly what Norma had advised us to avoid. The wisdom of her counsel was driven home to me month after month for *three years*, which was how long it took for our old house to sell.

Without consulting Norma, I told the builder, "Let's go ahead and get started, but let's keep it a secret."

Money also began to rule what I did with my time—and I resented it. I enjoyed speaking and writing, not sitting down for hours trying to manage all the aspects of financial planning, building, giving, being fair with my staff, and setting aside funds for future growth.

Our ministry was also growing. We hired more people, bought the latest and greatest equipment, and gave everyone raises and bonuses. None of these things were wrong, in and of themselves. But what was happening was that I was subtly and gradually depending less on God and relying more and more on my own wisdom and understanding. At the time it all seemed good: Not only were we taking in a lot of money, we were also giving away a lot of money to ministries and people in need.

Subtly and gradually, I was depending less on God and relying more and more on my own wisdom and understanding.

During this time, I began to develop newer, grander expectations, expectations that included much more growth. Worldwide growth. With the financial ability to do so many different things, we were constantly asking ourselves, "What should we do next? How can we make this better? How can we reach more people?"

As the ministry grew, I think I just assumed that everyone would work well together and be happy. And like a lot of people, I expected that the material blessings would add an extra measure of happiness to my life and my work. I expected life to be more fulfilling. But instead of experiencing greater fulfillment, I felt that I was constantly overwhelmed by deadlines and frustrated that other people were not being reliable in helping me manage my money and my ministry. If they didn't do things fast enough or well enough or just the way I wanted them done, I would come unglued. My actions and words didn't always match that of a Spirit-led Christian. Mostly I expressed myself by complaining, griping, and judging other people. I was totally ignoring God's truths, and I wasn't heeding his Word.

In my heart, I knew that God had given our ministry favor and that it wasn't by my own efforts we were being successful. But it didn't take long for me to forget this truth. I had prayed for all the big breaks through the years, and now the doors seemed to be opening automatically. I started expecting that life would keep getting better and that more and more doors to ministry would be opened. And I expected people to keep responding to me and to the message the same way they always had.

Through the years, my ego started to swell and pride settled in my heart. I never lost the awareness that God was the one who had opened all the doors for my ministry, but as people started treating me more graciously wherever I went, I began to expect compliments and accolades. No matter where I went, whether traveling for business in the United States and Europe or on vacation in Mexico, people would come up to me and say, "I bought your video, and it changed my life! My marriage has been saved. I just wanted to thank you." After a while, the attention became almost embarrassing, and I secretly hoped that no one would recognize me or interrupt me. I grew weary of the attention.

Tragically, I was tempted to believe that I was the one who had changed all these lives. I kept telling myself I was on the right track, because how else could all these good things happen? Why else would God bless me like this? I concluded that the overwhelming prosperity must be part of God's plan and the answer to my prayers. So I forged ahead.

As the ministry grew, I think I just assumed that everyone would work well together and be happy.

I kept telling myself I was on the right track, because how else could all these good things happen? Why else would God bless me like this?

People continued to treat me like a celebrity, and I began to act like one. I expected special treatment in restaurants and on airplanes, and I always traveled with an assistant to keep people from getting too close to me. How's that for a so-called relationship expert?

The Bible warns us about what can happen when we listen to too much flattery. Proverbs 29:5 says, "Whoever flatters his neighbor is spreading a net for his feet." The people who thanked me for my ministry weren't trying to set a trap for me, but I was beginning to think more highly of myself than I should have. I started believing all the hype. How blind I became!

All the attention and ego-stroking caused a disorientation in my soul. My perception of myself was out of whack, and I had a very skewed view of the worth of other people. My grandiose expectations continued to rule my life, and I became increasingly intolerant of anyone who didn't quite measure up.

One time one of my neighbors reacted to my attitude when we had a disagreement. She said, "Gary, you are nothing but a prima donna, and it's ugly." But that didn't faze me. I just figured she was jealous of my success. Such is the nature of pride. I was spoiled and self-centered, and it had happened so naturally and gradually that I hadn't even noticed. I didn't want to deal with any relational messes. I didn't want to deal with any inconveniences, and I resented anyone who tried to hold up my plans. I wanted my relationships with other people—including those with my staff and my family—to be hassle free and manageable.

Cracks in the Wall

By the mid-1990s, Norma and I had moved to Branson and had begun a new organization, the Smalley Relationship Center. My three children—Kari, Greg, and Michael—had become involved in the ministry, and all indications were that we would continue to grow and prosper. We had already accomplished more than I had ever dreamed of, yet my personal walk with God had grown progressively colder and more distant. I felt spiritually dead inside. My motivation to continue with my ministry was gone. I was discouraged and confused. Boy, was I confused!

My relationships were suffering severely. After delivering a message at one of my seminars on how to get over anger and stress, I headed back to the hospitality room with my two sons, who were sharing the speaking responsibilities with me. Just minutes after teaching about anger, I had a disagreement with Michael and Greg about something and I lost my temper. That was the pattern in my life at that time. I let all my negative thoughts control me.

I remember Greg stepping back and saying to me, "Dad, why don't you reread the book you wrote fifteen years ago called *Joy That Lasts.*" I felt the sting of his words, and it made me even more angry and irritated.

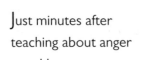

Just minutes after teaching about anger . . . I lost my temper.

I wasn't prepared to receive words of rebuke and correction from my son. But Greg had observed how people would come up to me after a seminar and tell me how much their relationships had been helped by my books or tapes, yet he knew I was not heeding my own counsel.

What my son said to me was true, though I didn't accept it at the time. I was embarrassed by his rebuke, but he was right! I honestly had forgotten what God had taught me fifteen years earlier—that Jesus is all I need. He is the source of all my joy.

The incident with Greg and Michael made me painfully aware of my relational bankruptcy. Looking back, I realize how my son's stern words were good medicine for me. As much as I had counseled and helped other families to get along, I was unable to work alongside my own sons. I was blinded by self-centeredness, unable to see the damage I was doing to the relationships around me. No wonder I felt so empty.

My whole life, it seemed, was consumed with pulsating stress. I was bothered by the traffic on my five-mile commute to work. I was irritated by the inconvenience of air travel from Branson to all my seminars. I was stressed by a steady series of publishing deadlines and the need to come up with new seminar material. I was worried about the weather as Norma and I were building our new house. And I was caught up in the tension of working together with family members in ministry. It seemed that everything was a hassle or a distraction, and everything cost more than I had anticipated. The pressure was becoming unbearable. Ironically, the things I had expected to bring me fulfillment and enjoyment in life turned out to be the very things that created havoc.

> My whole life, it seemed, was consumed with pulsating stress.

Out of the Frying Pan . . .

After 1995, I started slowing down my direct involvement at the Smalley Relationship Center and began working out a plan to transfer control of the ministry to my children over the next several years. In 1996, my book *Making Love Last Forever* was published and sold exceptionally well.

Seeing this success, several of my friends who had built their own thriving and profitable businesses told me that if I really wanted to move up the ladder and take my publishing venture to the next level, I should consider signing up with a New York literary agent who worked with all the top publishers and could get my book proposals in front of them. This particular agent was very good at taking individuals who had achieved fame and success in one field—people such as Dr. Phil McGraw, Maria Shriver, and Jake Steinfeld of *Body by Jake* fame—and helping them break into the publishing world. It sounded like a good idea to enlist her help.

With my next proposal, the agent took me to New York to visit three publishers. Eventually, we signed a two-book contract with Simon & Schuster. But now the pressure was really on. My books had been successful for years in the Christian market, but I felt that if I didn't hit a home run in the general market as well, I would be considered a failure.

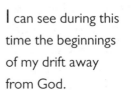

I can see during this time the beginnings of my drift away from God.

Looking back with the perspective of five or ten years, I can see during this time the beginnings of my drift away from God. I listened to the voices of other people telling me, "You've got to do this," "It only makes sense," "It's the next natural step," or "If you want to be successful . . ." I can see how these voices distracted me from depending on God for every part of my life.

Things really began to come to a head in 2000 with the publication of my first book with Simon & Schuster, *Secrets to Lasting Love.* To begin with, it wasn't the book I wanted to write. In fact, I had signed the contract based on another idea, but when I started to write that book, the publisher didn't like the direction it was taking and steered me toward the "secrets to lasting love" idea.

This felt like old news to me. My most recent book prior to that was *Making Love Last Forever,* and I felt as if I had already said everything I had to say on that particular subject. As I tried to write, I struggled internally and said to myself, "Smalley, you're not saying anything new, you're just saying it in a different way." But the publisher wouldn't budge.

My name had already slowed down in the marketplace because the infomercial I used to do had been off the air for a couple of years. When *Secrets to Lasting Love* didn't sell as well as expected, the situation went from bad to worse. I felt that my agent should be doing more to help me promote the book, but she said, "You told me you were going to have an infomercial, but you can't seem to work it out." And then Simon & Schuster said, "We're not sure we want to do the second book." It was a nightmare.

In the end, the contract was canceled and I walked away from a lot of money, but I was so happy to get away from that situation that I didn't care how much it cost me.

In the wake of all this, I started to think that whatever I was going to accomplish in life I had already done. I didn't have any new material to write about, and I didn't have any really big dreams. I decided that God must be done with me, or at least I was done with ministry. It was like I plateaued. I just *ended.*

> I started to think that whatever I was going to accomplish in life I had already done.

I sat in ministry meetings where everyone was discussing my retirement—or even more discouraging, discussing what would happen when I died! I began to believe I was done. I lost my vision for what God had called me to do. I lost my hunger for God's Word because I had lost sight of who I was. I went to church, but usually I would end up critiquing the sermon.

During this season of my life, I'm sure I prayed, but I don't remember any kind of routine. I'm sure I read my Bible, but I wasn't doing any kind of regular study. I wasn't reminding myself daily from God's Word of why I was here, what I was doing, and what my purpose in life was. I lost my ability to hope and dream. I drifted away from God and went my own way. I spent money, took trips, and got caught up in materialism again. God didn't seem to be giving me a new vision for what was next, so it seemed logical for me to scale back my involvement in the ministry, hand over the reins to my children, and help them get going.

If you've ever worked in a family business, you know where this story is headed.

An Unsuccessful Succession

All three of my children have very strong personalities. Before they joined the Smalley Relationship Center, they had already developed their own vision and their own ministries. So when we brought everyone together under one roof, they all had their own ideas of how we should operate and what we should do. Almost immediately, I realized I had made a big mistake in trying to have everyone work together. Trying to pull together four ministries in one and have all of us agree on a common direction was a recipe for conflict, misunderstanding, and confusion. We had a lot of very stressful family meetings trying to come to a win-win-win-win solution (remember, it was three kids and Dad) about the direction of the ministry.

After some of those family meetings, I was more stressed out than ever. We were usually a harmonious family who really enjoyed each other most of the time, but now we found ourselves at loggerheads. Despite our good intentions for serving people through our ministry and building a family enterprise, we were at each other's throats.

"I don't like your proposal."

"Oh yeah? Well, I don't like *your* proposal, and I don't like *you* all that much, either!"

I don't think anyone ever actually said that, but it seemed that was the tone of many of our meetings. On more than one occasion, I found myself thinking, *What have I gotten myself into?*

And then, as part of the generational succession plan, other members of the family became owners and voting members of the organization. All of a sudden, my children's spouses—wonderful people with whom I'd had great relationships, but mostly at family holiday gatherings—were standing up in meetings to voice their opinions about what we should do. I would sit there thinking, *This is like an out-of-body experience that I don't want to be a part of. What happened to my ministry?*

On more than one occasion, I found myself thinking, *What have I gotten myself into?*

As if all that wasn't stressful enough, my elder son, Greg, who had succeeded me as president of the ministry, decided he wanted more professional efficiency in our day-to-day operations as the counseling ministry grew. So he reassigned the office manager and put her in charge of making travel arrangements for our speakers. Well, the office manager just happened to be my wife, Norma, who had run the daily operations of the ministry for twenty years.

Greg handled the reassignment in a very loving and respectful way, but it still hurt, and Norma was very discouraged. She would glare at me and say, "You did this, Gary. You put him there. This was *your* idea."

If you've heard the saying, "If the momma ain't happy, ain't nobody happy," you have an idea of what things were like. I thought, *How did I make such a mess of everything, and what am I going to do about it?*

In his role as president, Greg talked to me about my contribution to the content of our seminars. He said, "Dad, you've got to come up with some new stuff when you speak at the big simulcast we're putting on in six months." But I didn't have anything new to say. All I had was a load of hurt from all the things that were happening with my family, and I was struggling with that. While we were teaching others how to have effective relationships, our own relationships were being tested to the core.

There were new financial pressures as well. Within the new ministry structure, we began to expand again, paying big-name speakers to be part of our simulcasts and adding counselors to our staff, which grew from thirteen to forty-three. These professional counselors were paid professional-level salaries, which meant a major increase in our overhead. To balance our cash flow during this expansion, we established a line of credit with the bank, but when our revenues didn't keep pace with what we were borrowing, the bank got nervous. Even though by now I was only one of several owners, the bank made it very clear that if the company got in financial trouble, they weren't going to go after my children. They were going to go after me, because they knew what kind of assets I had.

> While we were teaching others how to have effective relationships, our own relationships were being tested to the core.

I often reflect on this ten-year period of my life and wonder how I survived. Thankfully, God provided the wake-up call I needed. He knew I needed a crisis to shake me out of my preoccupation with myself.

YOUR RELATIONSHIP WITH GOD

1. Does a close relationship with God come naturally to you? What can you do to draw closer to God?

2. What priorities in your life do you feel you have placed above God?

3. On a scale from 1–10 (10 being the highest), rate your level of stress. How is your stress level affecting your relationship with God?

KEY VERSES: Read Matthew 19:16-26

Prayerfully consider what earthly things might be coming between you and the Lord. Consider how you identify with the Rich Young Man.

MAKING IT PERSONAL

List some aspects of your life that you need to surrender fully to God. What areas of your life are a struggle for you to turn over to him?

A SUDDEN AWAKENING

In April 2002, the day finally arrived for the big simulcast we had been planning. We had lined up some top speakers, including James Dobson, Josh McDowell, Dennis Rainey, and Beth Moore, and I was supposed to be the keynote speaker. But for months I had been asking myself, "What am I going to say?" I don't remember my speech going well at all—I was under too much stress.

The conference ended on a Saturday, and the next day I went to Greg's vacation home up in the Ozarks for some rest and relaxation. I knew that I was extremely tired. I was dragging and feeling sleepy. In fact, I went upstairs at one point to take a nap because I felt so exhausted. It was abnormal, but I just wrote it off as fatigue from the weekend conference.

On Monday, I went hunting with a friend. As we trekked out into the woods, we soon ran across some wild turkeys. I took aim with my rifle and fired a shot, and at the same instant, I was stricken with a massive heart attack. I think the turkey and I hit the ground at the same time.

Certain that I was dying, I prayed and thanked God for my life and my family. A tremendous peace came over me as I whispered to God that I'd see him in a few moments. Even though I had drifted away from him, I was still certain of his love for me. As I waited to die, my friend pulled the truck as close as he could to where I was lying, helped me into the passenger seat, and drove me to the hospital.

I wasn't able to breathe well, but I finally gathered enough strength to call Norma on my cell phone. When she said, "Hello," I tried to tell her what had happened and to let her know one last time that I loved her. She thought I was joking. Interrupting me, she said, "I have someone with me, Gary," and she put me on hold.

Oh, well, I thought, I'll tell her again when we meet in heaven.

Though the memory of our miscommunication still brings back a chuckle, it also reminds me of how far away from God I really was at that time.

> I had already changed my diet in order to decrease my chances of having a heart attack, but I hadn't done anything about the stress in my life.

When we got to the hospital, my cardiologist could not believe I had made it that far. He found 100 percent blockage in one of my main heart arteries and said that by all rights I should be dead. Miraculously, not only had I survived, but there also was no damage to my heart.

The men in my family have a history of heart problems. For several generations preceding mine, every Smalley male by his mid-fifties had either died of a heart attack or survived one. I had already changed my diet in order to decrease my chances of having a heart attack, but I hadn't done anything about the stress in my life.

Not long after I recovered, Norma and I took a vacation to Cancun, Mexico, and I had a second brush with death. As I describe in *The DNA of Relationships*, I went swimming in unsafe ocean conditions, was caught in an undertow, and almost drowned before I was rescued by an alert lifeguard.

These near-death experiences shook me for a while, but sadly, I didn't allow them to penetrate deep enough to shake me out of my self-centered lifestyle. I did not turn back to God and commit to his direction for my life.

As summer turned to fall, I began having trouble with my kidneys. The doctors speculated that the damage was related to the heart attack, when the blood flow to the kidneys was stopped for a period of time. I have also since learned about the effects of prolonged stress on the human body, and I can see that stress definitely played a role in the deterioration of my kidneys. This was right at the time when I was transferring control of the Smalley Relationship Center to my children, so the stress levels, as I've already mentioned, were spiking off the chart.

"**W**hy are you letting other people control how you feel? Why are you giving them that power over you?"

I made monthly trips to the doctor's office to have my kidney levels tested. Each month, it seemed, the doctor was a bit more concerned than he had been the previous month. "Eventually," he said, "you're going to need to start dialysis or have a kidney transplant."

During this time, Greg observed my out-of-control emotional responses and said to me, "Dad, why are you letting other people control how you feel? Why are you giving them that power over you?" He was trying to teach me some of the same principles being developed for use in our seminars and counseling sessions, but I was so fogged out by stress and so caught up with my own reactions that it didn't make sense to me. I thought, *What in the world is he saying?* In my mind, having a heart attack, failing kidneys, and a company in turmoil were good reasons to feel horrible. I was as close to burnout as I had ever been. How else was I supposed to feel?

Failing Kidneys and a Hardened Heart

As my kidney problems got worse, I gradually began to cry out to God, but my attitude was one of trying to cut a deal with him rather than submitting to his plan for my life. Because I had lived what appeared to be a charmed life for so long, I thought I was above having to go through serious trials. When the doctors told me that I would need a kidney transplant, I didn't want to be bothered. God had given me everything I had asked for in the past, and I knew he could instantly heal me. For the previous decade, it had seemed that whenever I asked for something, God granted my request. I assumed he would rescue me once again so that I could avoid the surgery.

I continued to put off a decision about my kidneys. Instead, I prayed, "Okay, God, I know you can heal my kidneys, so please just do it." I went to a church up in Springfield for prayer, and in my heart I was saying, *Okay, God, I know you're going to heal me. . . . I'm expecting you to heal me. . . . Come on, heal me!* I really wasn't interested in any other solution. I just wanted things my way. But each time I went to the doctor, the test results were worse than the month before.

> God wanted to do a transforming work in my life. He wanted to give me a new *heart,* a completely new perspective on life and faith.

In hindsight, I can see that God wanted to do a transforming work in my life. He wanted to give me a new *heart,* a completely new perspective on life and faith. The kidney problems were simply a means of bringing me to a place of submission to God. He had something much more radical and life saving in mind than just healing my kidneys.

Not only did I assume that God would rescue me, but I also hardened my heart to him on a number of levels. Several months before my surgery, an evangelist who had a healing ministry came to Branson. Somehow, he found out about my illness and came to my office to see me. He asked if he could pray for me, but I was not terribly interested in what he had to say. I had promised my grandkids that I would meet them at the lake that day, and all I could think about was getting out the door to see them. But I yielded to the evangelist's request and allowed him to pray for me. He invited Norma to join us, as well.

> I was irritated that he was taking so long, keeping me from being with my grandkids.

Before he prayed, he explained to me the biblical basis for healing. He must have talked for about fifteen minutes, but it seemed like an hour. Instead of appreciating his compassion and the fact that he had gone out of his way to visit me, I was irritated that he was preaching at me and that it was taking so long, keeping me from being with my grandkids.

Finally, I said abrasively, "I know what the Scripture says. Just start praying."

Sensing my unreceptive heart, he began to pray. But right in the middle of his prayer, as he was quoting various Scriptures, I said, "Okay, right, I get it." Norma kicked me under the table, but I was on a roll now. When the evangelist didn't take the hint and finish his prayer, I interrupted him again: "Okay, okay!"

Finally, I stood up and walked toward the door. "You can keep praying for me," I said, "but I've got to go. I'm late for meeting my grandkids."

Norma blushed with embarrassment, but the evangelist responded graciously to my unacceptable behavior. Now I'm embarrassed when I look back and see how deeply my heart had become hardened to what God was doing in my life.

Michael's Sacrificial Gift

It wasn't long before the function level of my kidneys had declined to a point where we started to talk seriously about a transplant and to look for donors. At that point, my three children—Michael, Greg, and Kari—stepped forward and offered to donate a kidney if theirs were compatible with mine. They were all tested and Kari's and Michael's were matches. The doctors chose Michael as the best overall candidate and asked, "When's the best time to do this?"

With my speaking schedule in 2003, the first available time wasn't until the end of November. The doctor said that he thought my kidneys would last until then, so we scheduled the surgery. I still wasn't reconciled to the idea of surgery—I continued bargaining with God right up until the weekend before the operation—but I didn't argue about it with my family or the doctors. I was preoccupied with problems in the ministry and preparing for a huge simulcast that was scheduled for the week before the surgery.

When November arrived, my kidney function had not improved and my stress level was dangerously high. After months of turmoil, I decided to take back ownership of the Smalley Relationship Center and reassert my control of the ministry. Greg stepped down as president and took over the counseling division, while I renewed my focus on the seminar division. As part of the transition, we released a number of employees. Those were tough, emotionally difficult days, and we all felt the effects of the transition.

Soon it was time for the transplant operation. I finished my part of the simulcast on a Saturday, and on Sunday I flew to Los Angeles for the surgery, which would happen the next day.

Reality set in when I arrived at the small, old hospital near downtown Los Angeles. Michael and I went through the pretesting, and I was apprehensive about everything. I knew that the doctors had come highly recommended, but I still found myself anxious about every aspect of the surgery. I didn't want to go through with it. Looking around, I noticed that the facility didn't seem to have some of the modern conveniences of other hospitals. The rooms were small, and the whole place seemed as if it could use a face-lift. My uneasiness about the whole ordeal heightened. I knew I was not prepared for the surgery, mentally or spiritually. I could hardly pray, and my focus was mainly on myself—pretty much where it had been for the past decade.

My worries about myself overshadowed my concern for Michael. Here he was generously offering me one of his kidneys, but the reality of his sacrifice didn't penetrate my heart. I knew it was an amazing gift, but I was too self-absorbed to appreciate it at the time, too distracted with my own worries.

On the morning of the surgery, before they rolled me to the surgery unit, Norma prayed for me and we kissed good-bye. Tears came to my eyes as I realized that it was possible I wouldn't survive the surgery. Even though I believed that my relationship with God was secure, I was not able to tap into his peace to help me through this trial.

The first part of the operation involved Michael. The doctors began by removing his kidney while I waited impatiently in the room next door. Little did I know that the size of Michael's kidney was causing complications. The doctors had to cut a rib to make room to get the kidney out. During this process, one of my son's lungs collapsed and his body began to shut down. While I was grumbling about the delay, the surgeons were working to keep my son alive. Thankfully, they were able to stabilize his condition, and the operation proceeded as planned.

> While I was grumbling about the delay, the surgeons were working to keep my son alive.

My portion of the surgery went very well, though I still had no idea that Michael had almost died. After the anesthesia wore off a bit, I remember waking up but still feeling incoherent and rather out of it. Norma's first words to me were, "Gary, Michael almost died from a collapsed lung." I can remember thinking, *Aren't you going to ask me how I'm feeling?* Sadly, I was still focused primarily on my own needs. Later, after the grogginess wore off, I asked more questions and found out more details about what had happened with Michael. He was still in a lot of pain, and the doctors had him on the strongest pain medication available; however, his condition was stable and the prognosis for his recovery was good.

As it turned out, Michael would bounce back fairly quickly, but I was headed for a long road of recovery. I was glad to be alive, but I still felt numb to a lot of things and indifferent about my relationship with God. My mind was still terribly distracted with the demands I felt were pressing in on my life. Although my body had survived the surgery, a part of me still felt dead.

Confronting My Deadly Emotions

After the surgery, I was especially susceptible to infection and therefore had to be quarantined. I had to wear a mask whenever anyone else was in the room, and I had to limit my activity to the bare minimum. I was tired, sore, grouchy, and depressed.

The day before I was scheduled to be discharged, a nurse came in to explain the medications I would have to take to keep my body from rejecting Michael's kidney. As soon as she walked into my room, I had her personality pegged. Her uniform was immaculate, her hair impeccable, her makeup flawless. She looked like she was going to a ball.

As one would expect from such a serious, detailed perfectionist, she went through every one of my forty medications and identified every one of the possible side effects. I was supposed to listen and take notes. Fortunately, my daughter, Kari, was there to take notes for me, because I could feel my stress level going through the roof.

If I experienced even half the side effects the nurse described, there wasn't much point in having had the transplant.

If I experienced even half the side effects the nurse described, there wasn't much point in having had the transplant. It seemed to me that I had survived the surgery only to die from the medications intended to heal me!

Kari and Norma tried to encourage me out of my black mood, but I just griped and complained. I griped about the nurses, griped about the food, griped about the care I was getting—I griped about anything and everything. In truth, some of the best doctors in the country had performed the transplant, and I had received excellent care, but none of this stopped me from grumbling.

After I was discharged from the hospital, I still needed regular follow-up care for about three weeks, so Norma and I checked into the Marriott Hotel five minutes away from the hospital. This gave me a fresh new set of circumstances to gripe about. Kari says I told her that junior high kids must run the world, because as far as I could see, nobody was responsible, nobody was professional, nobody did anything with excellence. Everybody forgot things and messed things up.

> As far as I could see, nobody was responsible, nobody was professional, nobody did anything with excellence.

One of the benefits of the surgery was that I had lost a lot of weight and thus, according to my doctor, I could eat whatever I wanted. So I ate lots of rice pudding—which I've always loved—and tapioca pudding. Tubs of it.

One day, Kari took me to the grocery store to pick up some medications and get some food. All the way to the store, I fussed and voiced my frustration. I was anxious about my recovery from the transplant, and I wasn't supposed to be out in public. The doctors had advised me not to get closer than ten feet to other people for at least three months. I had a mask on to protect me from coughs, sneezes, and other germs.

Kari parked in front of a large supermarket and hurried inside to get my prescriptions filled and to buy my groceries. Propped up in the backseat on a pillow, I nursed my complaining spirit, which only increased my stress.

Because of my susceptibility to infection, Kari left all the car windows up, but it was so hot that day in Southern California that it wasn't long before I was roasting. It was very difficult to move, but I finally was able to reach over the driver's seat and turn the key so I could lower the back windows and get some fresh air. I felt that Kari was taking too long, so I also griped about that.

As I was lying there, looking out the window, I became aware that the car was only about ten feet away from a line of picketers who were protesting outside the supermarket. They were yelling and screaming about how the grocery chain didn't pay them enough and telling people not to shop there. Their children were with them, coughing and crying, and I thought, *What was Kari thinking parking so close to these people?* I became upset that she had not been more concerned for *me*. My expectations of Kari were pretty unrealistic, and they definitely controlled my emotions.

When Kari—*finally!*—returned to the car, heavy laden with everything on my list and looking relieved to get back to me, I lashed out at her. Before she even had time to get into the car, I was scolding her. Instead of thanking her for helping me with my errands, I said, "How could you leave me out here so close to all these people who could infect me?"

She patiently responded, "Dad, if I'm going to care for you over the next several days, could I ask you to say 'please and thank you' instead of griping and complaining? I know that you have certain needs now, but it would be so much easier if you would be more kind and considerate of me."

> My expectations were pretty unrealistic, and they definitely controlled my emotions.

I shot back with a cutting remark about how much pain it was to go through this experience and how she should allow me to complain a little.

When we got back to the hotel, Kari dropped me off in my room with my tapioca pudding and other supplies. By now, she and Norma were so fed up with my attitude that they just needed to get away for a while. "We're going shopping," Norma said.

Of course, I griped about that, too. "What if I need something?" I muttered.

"Get it yourself. We'll be back."

After I got through complaining about "being abandoned," I sat on the bed alone, trying to watch TV, but there was nothing that caught my interest. I turned off the TV and tried to read the Bible, but I didn't want to read the Bible. I didn't know what to do with myself. I felt disgusted—I knew I was a complainer and probably hard to live with—but I didn't know how to act any different. I was restless and bored, and I could feel the stress building. As I shifted impatiently, trying to get more comfortable on my array of propped-up pillows, I noticed a book on the nightstand. It was a book that would change my life.

My Revival

The Friday before surgery, I had been in Norma's office and noticed a book on a table near her desk: *Deadly Emotions*, by Dr. Don Colbert. It's not uncommon for publishers to send me books that they hope I will endorse and promote through my ministry. I wasn't reading anything in particular at the time, and the book looked interesting, so I picked it up and took it home.

Later, when I packed my carry-on for the flight to Los Angeles, I had looked for something to read on the flight. *Deadly Emotions* was on the corner of my home office desk, so I tossed it into my bag.

I didn't read the book on the plane, and somehow it ended up on my nightstand at the hospital. During the first few days after my surgery, I had no interest in reading, but I saw the book now and then when I glanced in that direction.

Now, at the Marriott, there was the book again, on the nightstand. I don't know how it got there. Neither my wife nor my daughter remembered putting it there (so it wasn't as if they were trying to send me a message), but there it was. I was desperate for something to do, and because it was the only book I had with me, I decided to give it a try.

The book jacket listed some "deadly emotions" that cause dis-ease: bitterness, resentment, anxiety, and repressed anger. I began to reflect on my own burdensome emotions and felt drawn to see what this author had to say.

Within thirty pages, I was hooked. Dr. Colbert explained what stress is and how we can catch all kinds of dis-eases if we live with too much stress. He explained how my out-of-control, stress-filled life was killing my body one organ at a time. "And," he said, as if speaking directly to me, "if you don't manage your stress, you're going to be dead."

My out-of-control, stress-filled life was killing my body one organ at a time.

For some reason, Dr. Colbert's words cut straight to my heart in a way that nothing else had been able to do for years. Overwhelmed with conviction, I dropped to my knees and cried out, "God, I am fed up with all the stress in my life. I can't live this way anymore. I need your wisdom to know how to control my stress." Over the next twenty-four hours, I started to see my life for what it really was, and I knew that I couldn't go back to the same de-structive lifestyle.

Dr. Colbert explained that stress is the gap between what we expect and what we experience. He recommends that we write down all of our expecta-tions so that we can begin to see where these gaps are occurring.

I started to see my life for what it really was, and I knew that I couldn't go back to the same destructive lifestyle.

When I finished the book, I could not wait to get down on my knees again and pray. I confessed to God that, even though I knew better, I had been caught up in my own agenda for my life. I asked him to forgive me. I knew that I needed his grace and power to help pull me out of my spiritual decline.

When I finished praying, I wrote my list of expectations, and with tears and conviction and overwhelming emotion, I surrendered them, one-by-one, to God. It was just like an old-time revival meeting, right there in my room at the Marriott. I felt very much like the Prodigal Son, coming home to his forgiving father. As I read and reread passages of Scripture, the words seemed to cut through my heart, and God's Word became alive to me again. I burst into tears, thanking God not just for giving me a second chance but also for sparing my life three times. My once-lonesome hotel room felt like my own private altar, where I could call on the Lord and be in his presence.

> I startled myself by thinking of all the people I had hurt because of the selfish expectations I had placed on them.

When Norma returned to the room, I told her everything that God had shown me about myself. I asked for her forgiveness for how my attitudes had affected our marriage and our family.

Even I was shocked by the immediate transformation in my life. I didn't think a person could change that fast. On a scale of one to ten, my stress level went from a solid ten to almost zero. My heart was filled with gratitude and new hope. I felt as if I had a new lease on life.

With a lot of alone time on my hands while I recovered from the kidney transplant surgery, I startled myself by thinking of all the people I had hurt because of the selfish expectations I had placed on them. I prayed, "Lord, forgive me for how I have been treating people, and thank you for lifting the scales from my eyes."

Immediately, I thought of the last person I had treated poorly—my daughter, Kari. I knew that she had sacrificed time with her husband and children in order to come to California to help Norma care for me after the surgery. I remembered how irritable and hostile I had been when she took me to the grocery store, and it made me sick to realize what I had done.

No longer blinded by self-pity, I was finally able to see and appreciate God's gracious provision for my needs through my wife, my daughter, and the rest of my family.

Kari continued to serve me as she always had, and now I had no desire to complain or gripe. She knew that something in me had drastically changed. I felt a renewed compassion for my family. I felt as if I had self-control for the first time in years. God knew that I needed to feel this way so that I could heal properly. My haughtiness turned to meekness. My ingratitude turned to humility. My impatience turned to forgiveness.

> The most astonishing thing was that all I had to do was open my arms and receive this radical change as a gift from God.

The most astonishing thing was that all I had to do was open my arms and receive this radical change as a gift from God. I did nothing to earn it. I just followed the instructions that I found in Colossians 3, to set my heart on things above, not on earthly things.

Along with this transformation came a renewed desire to read and memorize Scripture. I started by memorizing Colossians 3:1-17, which gives a tremendous "before and after" picture of the Christian life.

I went on to memorize other passages of Scripture, as well, and each one added to my renewed perspective toward God:

Fix these words of mine in your hearts and minds; tie them as symbols on your hands and bind them on your foreheads. Teach them to your children, talking about them when you sit at home and when you walk along the road, when you lie down and when you get up. Write them on the doorframes of your houses and on your gates, so that your days and the days of your children may be many in the land that the LORD swore to give your forefathers, as many as the days that the heavens are above the earth. (Deuteronomy 11:18-21)

I have hidden your word in my heart
    that I might not sin against you.
Praise be to you, O LORD;
    teach me your decrees.
With my lips I recount
    all the laws that come from your mouth.
I rejoice in following your statutes
    as one rejoices in great riches.
I meditate on your precepts
    and consider your ways.
I delight in your decrees;
    I will not neglect your word. (Psalm 119:11-16)

Your word is a lamp to my feet and a light for my path.
    (Psalm 119:105)

God met me where I was and showed me how to renew my relationship with him. After years of wandering in the wilderness of my own selfish ways, I saw an overnight transformation in my life. My blood pressure dropped into the normal range, and the overwhelming stress I had felt for so long just disappeared. Finally, I began to understand what my son Greg had been trying to teach me. I wept at the depth of his love for me and thanked God that he had given Greg the courage to stand up to me and tell me what I needed to hear, even though my heart at the time was hardened.

As my recovery progressed, I woke up every morning to find out if my feeble old body was continuing to accept the new kidney. Each day, I grew stronger. Each day, I received fresh insight into God's Word and the work of the Holy Spirit. Healing was taking place physically and spiritually. On the one hand, I was still worn out, and I was tired of taking more than one hundred pills a day and adapting to the drugs' effects on my system. On the other hand, I was like a newborn baby who craved "pure spiritual milk."[1] I felt like a new Christian.

As God spoke clearly to my heart, he led me to focus again on Colossians 3:1-17. This section of Scripture was the catalyst for my transformation, and it gave me the insight I needed to remain faithful to the steps of recovery that God set before me. Because I had no distractions to worry about during this time, I was able to allow Scripture to really penetrate my heart and mind. Through prayer and my time in the Scriptures, I developed several new habits that shaped my renewed relationship with God. I learned how to surrender all my expectations to God and accept his filter for my life. I learned how to take every thought captive, according to 2 Corinthians 10:5, and I learned how to worship God in the midst of trials. I also learned the importance of seeking godly counsel in decision making and of reviewing God's promises to me every day.

When I surrendered my expectations and my agenda to God, he faithfully showed me how to grow in my relationship with him. I knew that the work he was doing in my heart was a process and that I needed to commit myself to a daily time of communication with him. He gave me the passion and the motivation to seek him first every day. Now, several years down the road, I can honestly say that my relationship with God is better than ever.

In the next six chapters, I will describe how God rekindled my appetite for studying his Word and how he taught me six new habits that have become a part of my daily life. Every morning when I wake up and every night before I go to bed, I consciously and deliberately review these new ways of thinking about my relationship with God, myself, and other people. With God's help, they have made all the difference for me. I believe they can make a difference for you, as well. Let me show you how.

YOUR RELATIONSHIP WITH GOD

1. Can you identify any "deadly emotions" that have taken control of your life?

2. Can you identify trials in your life that God may be using to get your attention?

KEY VERSES: Ezekiel 36:26-27
Ask God to give you a "heart of flesh."

MAKING IT PERSONAL
Confess to God any areas of your life that you have not been willing to surrender to him. Ask him to show you how to grow in your relationship with him.

part two

RENEWAL

3

SURRENDERING ALL
EXPECTATIONS TO GOD

When God broke through my hardened heart and began to transform my attitudes, I realized that the first thing that had to change were my expectations. I had to face up to the fact that my own sense of how things ought to be had come to rule my life and my emotions. It wasn't that the expectations themselves were wrong—we all have expectations; they're a natural part of life—but my expectations were all *Gary* centered rather than God centered.

I believe that God had me start by surrendering all my expectations to him because my unfulfilled expectations were the cause of much of the stress in my life and because they were distracting me from my relationship with God. God called me to let go of all my aspirations so that I could focus on him.

God promises that he will meet all our needs "according to his glorious riches in Christ Jesus."[1] Scripture doesn't say he'll meet *some* of our needs; it says he'll meet *all* our needs. I had read this verse countless times over the years, but I wasn't living according to what it promises. I was driven by my own agenda, my own goals, and my own good ideas. When I started to trust God fully and really believed he was faithful, I began to experience true peace. This, I believe, is what caused my stress level to drop so dramatically.

"Not my will, but yours be done"

Before I could surrender my expectations, I had to know what they were. I was able to name several right away, but many others I had never even put into words. I just had this gnawing sense that things weren't turning out the way I wanted them to. I had a lot of unspoken expectations of other people—and I just *expected* them to know what they were.

When I sat down and wrote out all my expectations, the list ran to four pages. I broke the list down into sixteen categories, including expectations for my publishing ventures, speaking engagements, ministry at the Smalley Relationship Center, travel schedule, money and possessions, reputation, and family. When I reviewed my list, I could see that what I really wanted—what I had come to *expect*—was that my life would be smooth, successful, and hassle free. I wanted to be in control, I wanted people to think highly of me, and I wanted all my plans to work out according to my timing.

To surrender my expectations to God, I spoke each one out loud and imagined myself setting it at the foot of the cross. Confessing my expectations to God was eye-opening. I couldn't believe how they had gained such a hold on me.

Giving up my expectations doesn't mean I no longer care about what happens. Far from it! What it means is that I care more about what *God* wants to accomplish than what *I* want to accomplish. It means that I'm willing to set aside my own agenda, my own hopes and dreams, my own purposes and plans in order to pursue

God's agenda, God's purpose, and God's plan for my life. It means that God's expectations become my expectations.

Giving up my expectations means I'm willing to set aside my own ego, pride, comfort, and sense of ownership and accomplishment in order to glorify God. I learned that I need to adopt the same attitude that Jesus expressed in the garden of Gethsemane when he prayed for the cup of sacrifice to be taken from him: "Father . . . not my will, but yours be done."[2]

> Giving up my expectations means I'm willing to set aside my own ego, pride, comfort, and sense of ownership and accomplishment in order to glorify God.

It wasn't easy for Jesus to set aside his own will in the garden of Gethsemane. He knew it would cost him his life! The Bible says that the anguish of this decision caused his sweat to be "like drops of blood falling to the ground."[3] And though my decision was nothing compared to the sacrifice that Christ made, I soon found that it wasn't going to be easy for me to set aside my expectations.

Put to the Test

Less than a year after my kidney transplant, my willingness and ability to surrender my expectations to God were put to a severe test. I tell this story as an example of how our own expectations can take over again relatively quickly, even after we've surrendered them to God, and of how God allows our expectations to be cut down again so that we'll continue to trust in him alone. You see, when you surrender your expectations to God, you have to be willing to accept that his plan may not go according to what you hoped or expected. Ultimately, God wants all of us to learn that he is trustworthy and that his plan is best. It's a hard lesson to learn, and I'm still learning it.

Well before the kidney transplant, toward the end of 2000, I had signed a multibook deal with Tyndale House Publishers. Together with their editors, my ministry staff, and my family, I started working on a major ten-year plan for my ministry, which was to include films, TV, books, curriculum, and other innovative ministry opportunities. I've always loved dreaming big, and this campaign was going to be bigger than anything we had ever done.

> I've always loved dreaming big, and this campaign was going to be bigger than anything we had ever done.

Along with my publisher, I worked with a talented team of visionaries and strategic thinkers to create a plan for how to reach thousands of pastors, churches, and denominational leaders around the world with our new marriage material. As part of the plan, we were introduced to an organization that had experience in marketing directly to churches. This group was going to help us get our products into some new sales channels and develop an umbrella campaign that we hoped would tie together all the pieces of the plan.

By 2003, my sons and I had written several nonfiction books for Tyndale, and I had collaborated with novelist Karen Kingsbury on a fiction series, which sold very well. But by then, the rest of the campaign was starting to encounter some trouble. This coincided with the low point of my "black period" leading up to the kidney transplant. The pressure was overwhelming, and tensions were running high between me and several members of the team. Looking back, I can see that some of my expectations were unrealistic, and the way I related to people was often antagonistic. As I explain in *The DNA of Relationships*, my two main core fears are of being controlled by others and being belittled. During the course of developing this campaign, my buttons got pushed more than once, and I responded negatively. Ultimately, we parted ways with the strategic planning organization and had to give up the direct-to-church concept.

This change of direction at first seemed devastating. We had put a lot of time and energy into the various pieces of the campaign, and now, suddenly, the direct-to-church portion of the plan wasn't going to happen. But we still had a major new book in development, and we quickly regrouped around the efforts of a topflight marketing company that was brought in to help redirect the campaign. Their expertise was in media placement and public relations, so we decided to focus less on churches and instead developed a national media campaign (we were still hopeful that we could reach many of the same pastors we had targeted for the direct-to-church effort). Once again, we were dreaming big, and I was hopeful and thrilled about the campaign we put together, which was set to roll out in the fall of 2004. My expectations were once again built up, and now would come the real test of whether I was willing to surrender my expectations to God.

> This change of direction at first seemed devastating. We had all put a lot of time and energy into the various pieces of the campaign, and now, suddenly, this portion of the plan wasn't going to happen.

As the campaign kickoff date in 2004 drew nearer, it became apparent that the media promotion was not coming together as planned. There was a lot happening around the world at that time, and we were competing for airtime with some heavy issues, including the presidential election, the war in Iraq, and ongoing terrorism concerns. For a variety of reasons, the marketing company was unable to promote my book according to plan. And when the marketing efforts fell short of expectations, it was like one leg of a three-legged table collapsing; all the other pieces of the campaign, which were tied to the success of the marketing, came crashing down.

I was devastated. I felt lower than a snake's belly. Even though I had made huge spiritual strides since the kidney transplant, my first response to this jarring turn of events was self-pity, grave disappointment, embarrassment, and humiliation. I wanted to crawl into bed, curl up in the fetal position, and shut out the world. Once again, I thought that my ministry days were over. The four years of planning seemed like a waste of energy and time (others on the team must have felt the same way).

I grieved over this loss for three months. I felt as if I had been fired from my dream job. I would fall asleep grieving, wake up in the morning hurting, and feel sick several times during the day. My stomach, heart, and head ached. I remember saying to myself, "Is this where my career has taken me, to a dead-end road?" After this huge failure in my life, I had no idea what to plan for the future, and I now found it harder to trust people. And yet, God seemed to be asking, "Will you trust *me?*"

Removing Self-Imposed Restrictions

This crushing setback turned out to be the crucible in which I learned to wake up every morning and surrender my expectations to God. I had the sense that God was saying, "Gary, I want to prove to you that I am in charge and I am 100 percent enough for you, but I have to work your old way of thinking out of you." I finally realized that I could choose to suffer by holding on to my expectations and self-imposed restrictions, or I could choose to surrender everything to God. I chose to surrender! As I began to take responsibility for my actions and my choices, I automatically stopped blaming circumstances and other people for my unhappiness. My emotions were no longer held captive to the actions of other people, and they no longer had the same power over me. Sure, I still had my moments when I would revert to old patterns of behavior, but I began to realize that I was the one creating all my unreasonable expectations, and therefore I could stop. I could change.

A few years have passed since this experience, but it is still very real to me today. This life-changing "attitude adjustment" took root at the very core of my being. It now colors everything I do and sets the tone of my service to God. Every morning before I get out of bed, I recommit myself to renewing my mind through the principles found in Colossians 3. Since my experience back in 2003, I have spent a great deal of time meditating on these verses, deepening my understanding of them. I have become what I think about day and night. I have the peace of God flowing in my heart.

> I began to realize that I was the one creating all my unreasonable expectations, and therefore I could stop. I could change.

I now understand what went wrong with the last ten years of my life, where all the negative emotions came from, and why such pressure was building up inside of me. Through the difficult struggles with my health, God was able to get my attention and show me what needed to change. My thoughts are what caused my continual stress. I was responsible for what was happening to me—no one and nothing else. Wow, did it ever wake me up when I realized I could no longer blame circumstances or other people for my level of stress and my emotional condition!

What unrealistic expectations are you hanging on to? Are they distracting you from pursuing your relationship with God? Are they messing up your relationships with other people? Are they creating unhealthy stress in your life? My prayer is that you would learn how to surrender your expectations to God every day and that love for God would take over your heart and give you a greater sense of his peace. This freedom is available to everyone. It's available to you.

> I realized I could no longer blame circumstances or other people for my level of stress and my emotional condition.

Perhaps as you are reading this right now, you're saying to yourself, "Well, that's great for you, Gary. I'm glad you had your spiritual transformation and that things have turned around for you, but you don't know my situation. You don't know my struggles, my thought life, or the kind of stress I endure every day." If that summarizes your response, let me offer you some encouragement. I definitely believe this message is for you.

Your temptations, expectations, and stresses may not be the same as mine. But the solution is the same, because God never changes. He has given us his written Word to remind us that he himself is the solution to all of life's concerns. When I have negative emotions or I'm unhappy or discouraged, I go right back to the Word of God. I have fifteen or twenty verses that I review every day to keep my mind and my emotions on the right track. Here are just a few:

> Not only so, but we also rejoice in our sufferings, because we know that suffering produces perseverance; perseverance, character; and character, hope. And hope does not disappoint us, because God has poured out his love into our hearts by the Holy Spirit, whom he has given us. (Romans 5:3-5)

[The Lord] said to me, "My grace is sufficient for you, for my power is made perfect in weakness." Therefore I will boast all the more gladly about my weaknesses, so that Christ's power may rest on me. That is why, for Christ's sake, I delight in weaknesses, in insults, in hardships, in persecutions, in difficulties. For when I am weak, then I am strong. (2 Corinthians 12:9-10)

Consider it pure joy, my brothers, whenever you face trials of many kinds, because you know that the testing of your faith develops perseverance. Perseverance must finish its work so that you may be mature and complete, not lacking anything. (James 1:2-4)

Do not merely listen to the word, and so deceive yourselves. Do what it says. (James 1:22)

I encourage you to become grounded in the Word of God. Review God's promises on a daily basis. I've found that when I review these verses (and others) every day, they're enough to remind me of who I am, who empowers me, who has given me life, and who continues to give me life.

Maybe you are struggling with a specific addiction (whether it's to a substance, a pattern of thinking, or a way of life) that is consuming you and distracting you from God. Again, this message is for you. I have found freedom from addiction to the compulsions in my life, and I am no longer enslaved to temptation. (It doesn't mean I'm not tempted; but I am no longer a slave to temptation.) I sincerely believe that you, too, can experience such freedom. Psychiatrist Dr. Gerald May has said that "all addictions are medication for the pain of unfulfilled and conflictive relationships."[4] When your relationship with Christ becomes real and alive (which brings true fulfillment), the addictive nature starts to fade.

I pray that the story of my own spiritual fall might save you from losing what I lost. Perhaps God is calling you to examine your heart right now. What expectations or other points of stress can you identify that are pulling you away from God? Will you surrender them to God right now? I don't want you to waste another moment living outside of God's best for you. I've written a lot of books over the years, and they have all been important messages that I felt God wanted me share with others. But few times have I been as eager as I am right now to share what God has laid on my heart. I've made some big mistakes, and I've learned firsthand that there's a price to pay for drifting away from God. But I've also learned a lot about the grace of God and that he always gives us a chance to turn back to him.

> What expectations or other points of stress can you identify that are pulling you away from God? Will you surrender them to God right now?

YOUR RELATIONSHIP WITH GOD

1. Examine the expectations you carry around with you daily. Make a list of expectations you have that are unhealthy, unrealistic, and self-serving.

2. What expectations do you have that are healthy and God centered? Make a list, and compare it with your list of unhealthy expectations. Which list is longer?

3. On a scale of 1–10 (10 being the highest), how much are your expectations contributing to your stress level?

KEY VERSES: Read Matthew 6:25-34
Meditate on how you could seek God's Kingdom rather than your own

personal expectations. Take a moment to pray for strength and wisdom to let go of things that are hindering your relationship with God.

MAKING IT PERSONAL

Memorize Matthew 6:33-34. Make a point of meditating on these verses when you feel yourself wanting to be driven by negative expectations. Find a friend who will pray with you as you set godly priorities and increase your God-centered list of expectations.

4

TAKING EVERY
THOUGHT CAPTIVE

When I was growing up, I compared myself with other people and often ended up feeling inferior. For example, I believed that my academic skills were below par. I didn't do well on school tests, I was a slow reader, and I couldn't spell a thing. Embarrassed most of the time in class with my school friends, I concluded that I was a dummy. Of course, it didn't help my self-image that I had failed the third grade. My kids used to bend over in laughter when they'd hear my story—"Dad, how does anyone flunk third grade?"—and I'd laugh with them, but you can bet it wasn't funny when I was a kid.

I'll never forget the day when I realized that my slow academic mind was actually an asset for me. Because I tend to think simply and practically, I also tend to write and teach in simple, practical ways that are easy for people to grasp. My struggles in school have actually made me a better writer and speaker, and more sensitive to my audience. When writing a book like this one, I take care to make sure it is easy to read and understandable to me. I figure if I can get it, almost anyone can.

I'm convinced that God can use anyone to communicate his truth. Nothing is impossible with God. But if I had continued to believe that I wasn't smart enough or that I had nothing to offer, I never would have attempted to write books and conduct seminars. And I would still be feeling discouraged, worthless, and "not good enough."

Here is one of the greatest truths I have learned along the way: People and circumstances do not control our responses; rather, it is what we believe that causes us to react, speak, and behave the way we do.

> People and circumstances do not control our responses; rather, it is what we believe that causes us to react, speak, and behave the way we do.

Pause and reflect on that statement for a moment. When something happens to you, good or bad, what happens in your thought life? It's easy to fall into the trap of thinking that other people or our circumstances determine our emotions and our moods. However, what really controls our thought patterns is what we have buried deep inside of us—our core belief system, what the Bible calls our *heart*. It's what we believe in the deepest part of our being—about ourselves, about life, and about God—that determines how we think about and respond to our circumstances.

In 2005, I spoke at a large church in Kansas City, Missouri. When I finished, I walked behind the stage to retrieve my carry-on case, cell phone, and n-CPAP breathing machine, which I use at night to relieve sleep apnea. All I saw was the breathing machine; my carry-on and cell phone were gone. I immediately started thinking about what was in my luggage and how expensive my cell phone was. I thought about the fortieth anniversary gifts I had purchased for my wife, my brand-new tennis shoes, my computer (with all my notes that I hadn't backed up), and my seminar material. These things were irreplaceable!

"This can't be happening!" I said to myself. "How could someone take my stuff in a church?"

I began to feel horrible. The upbeat mood I had brought with me from the seminar now plummeted into deep anxiety. Why? Because the circumstances indicated that someone had stolen my property, and I felt violated. I kept telling myself, "Bad things are happening to me. . . . I'm a victim. . . . People who do these things are terrible people. Why me, God?" I was definitely worried that I'd never again see my computer, the gifts, and my cell phone. My initial feelings were normal reactions that anyone might have in a similar situation.

On the way to the airport, I paused and thought about my attitude and decided to change my thinking.

For a short period of time, I allowed my thoughts about my circumstances to dictate my mood. But on the way to the airport, I paused and thought about my attitude and decided to change my thinking. I said to myself, "Hey, Smalley, what do you really believe about trials, and this one in particular?"

"Well, I believe that trials make me more like God, they give me more of his character, they teach me about his love, they give me more of his power, and they cause me to grow in maturity."

"Okay, so why are you so upset if what just happened has the potential to drive you closer to God? All that you lost was of only temporal value anyway."

I started meditating on some Bible verses that speak about God's faithfulness toward me, and I focused my mind on the positive aspects of my relationship with God. For the rest of the afternoon and evening—and also when I woke up at night with a worried, sick stomach—I tried to remember all the positive ways that God could work this out for good. In the midst of my worry and pain, I talked to God and said something like this: "God, this feels like a really weighty trial to me, like there should be a gold medal waiting for me if I endure this hardship. But you are all the reward I need. Thank you for the privilege of suffering and for the new character I'm gaining through this pain (which is better than any gold medal), and for the added power you've given to me through it. I'm looking forward to seeing the changes in me."

I started meditating on some Bible verses that speak about God's faithfulness toward me, and I focused my mind on the positive aspects of my relationship with God.

Looking back, I realize that I was receiving good things from God even while I was grieving. I felt discouraged when it first happened—which is a normal response when something bad happens—but I didn't just wallow in my discouragement like I might have done in the past. Still, I didn't surrender it over to God as soon as I would have liked. I wish I could say that I immediately went to God's Word and to prayer and was no longer upset, but at first I had a hard time moving beyond myself. It's a learning process, and I'm still maturing and growing.

By morning, I felt great again. My mood had changed overnight. I was able to let the lost possessions go and started thinking about how I would replace them. I realized that everything I had was ultimately God's, and I was just a steward of all he had given me.

Through the course of events, I saw how much my thoughts influenced my moods. At the outset, my thoughts were centered on temporal things, my possessions. But I also realized how my thoughts could actually change what I believed to be true. When I took my thoughts "captive" by reminding myself of God's faithfulness and his other promises, I opened the door to allow God to heal my emotions and my mood. Remember, as our thoughts change over time, our whole lives change, including our emotions, words, actions, and even our outlook on life.

Renewing Your Mind Can Change Your Heart

"We take captive every thought to make it obedient to Christ."[1] If I had been living according to this truth ten years ago, I would not have been distracted by my success. Perhaps you've heard the expression, "You are what you think." Well, this is actually a biblical concept. The apostle Paul admonishes us to capture all our thoughts and bring them into submission to Christ so that our entire beings will be fully subject to Christ's lordship. In 1 Corinthians 2:16, Paul makes a bold statement, telling us that "we have the mind of Christ." This doesn't mean we are all-wise, all-knowing, and all-powerful like God. Rather, as we bring our thoughts into submission to Christ, our minds are molded into his likeness and we can discern spiritual truth.

Focusing my mind on Christ, taking every thought captive to him, is easier said than done. I want to keep my mind focused on him, but I get very busy and (with my personality) very distracted. Perhaps you've heard the saying, "Hurry, worry, bury," which refers to our tendency to run ourselves into the ground. Does that describe your life? I know it does mine.

I remember being asked to speak at a national pastor's conference in Atlanta. I was scheduled to do the final presentation of the three-day conference on Saturday afternoon. I had spent many hours in preparation for a forty-five-minute session, and that afternoon I was excited to share my message. But something was going wrong for me: The conference was breaking into a revival atmosphere, and the worship segment was running overtime as it seemed to be supernaturally led.

By the time the conference schedule was an hour behind, I was focusing on how frustrating it would be not to give my message. I must have looked at my watch every other minute, trying to calculate how this was ever going to work. I even asked the conference leader, "What are you going to do?" My attitude was 100 percent focused on myself, my reputation, and the message I had prepared. Surely with all the time I had spent they needed to hear my message.

And then, in the midst of what God was doing, it hit me: He doesn't wear a watch! Let me say that again: God does not wear a watch. I heard God's still, small voice say, "Smalley, I am doing a mighty work here today. Are you with me or against me?"

To focus our minds on Christ, we must slow down and get quiet in our worship.

I learned an important lesson that day. When the conference leaders asked me to close the session with my message, I told them I believed that God had already spoken through the events of the day and nothing else needed to be said. Instead, all the speakers went to the podium together and led a time of prayer and summary of what God had done that day.

To focus our minds on Christ, we must slow down and get quiet in our worship. We must set aside our time-clock mentality and get in tune with the rhythm of God's work in the world. Paul writes, "Be very careful, then, how you live—not as unwise but as wise, making the most of every opportunity, because the days are evil."[2] When we take every thought captive to Christ, we will live wisely, making the most of every opportunity the Lord provides.

We live in a world that is rejecting God more and more. Every day, we are inundated with cultural messages that run contrary to God's Word. That's why it is so important that we renew our minds daily through the truth found in Scripture. Romans 12:2 says, "Do not conform any longer to the pattern of this world, but *be transformed by the renewing of your mind.* Then you will be able to test and approve what God's will is—his good, pleasing and perfect will" (emphasis added).

How can we renew our minds? By focusing on God's transforming truth. How much time do you spend thinking about the things of this world? How much time do you spend meditating on God's Word and setting your mind on things above? Here are the verses I have used to bring my negative, worldly thoughts into submission to Jesus Christ:

> Finally, brothers, whatever is *true,* whatever is *noble,* whatever is *right,* whatever is *pure,* whatever is *lovely,* whatever is *admirable*—if anything is *excellent* or *praiseworthy*—*think about such things.* Whatever you have learned or received or heard from me, or seen in me— put it into practice. *And the God of peace will be with you.* (Philippians 4:8-9, emphasis added)

I encourage you to meditate on these verses, and don't miss the promise at the end: "The God of peace will be with you." God promises his peace—and his presence—if we will focus our minds on the eight powerful words in this passage and practice what we have learned.

Take some time to examine your thought life in light of Philippians 4:8-9. Are your thoughts and beliefs *true, noble, right, pure, lovely, admirable, excellent,* and *praiseworthy?* If you find that your beliefs and thoughts don't line up with these verses, it's time to change your beliefs and edit your thoughts to bring them in line. It's just that simple.

There are many other Scriptures that deal specifically with our thought life, but here are some verses that have helped to transform my thoughts:

- "The thief comes only to steal and kill and destroy; I have come that they may have life, and have it to the full."[3] Fullness of life is available *now*, for all who accept Jesus as their Lord.

- "I pray that out of his glorious riches he may strengthen you with power through his Spirit in your inner being, so that Christ may dwell in your hearts through faith. And I pray that you, being rooted and established in love, may have power, together with all the saints, to grasp how wide and long and high and deep is the love of Christ, and to know this love that surpasses knowledge—that you may be filled to the measure of all the fullness of God. Now to him who is able to do immeasurably more than all we ask or imagine, according to his power that is at work within us, to him be glory in the church and in Christ Jesus through-out all generations."[4] We don't have to do things in our own strength, because God can do immeasurably more than we can ask or think.

- "He gives us more grace. That is why Scripture says: 'God opposes the proud but gives grace to the humble.' Submit yourselves, then, to God. Resist the devil, and he will flee from you. Come near to God and he will come near to you."[5] God gives grace to the humble. A humble person is one who recognizes his or her helplessness without God. It may seem like an impossible task to control our thoughts, but when we admit that we are weak, we make room for God's strength to take over. There is room for God to work in us when we are humble.

- "My dear brothers, take note of this: Everyone should be quick to listen, slow to speak and slow to become angry, for man's anger does not bring about the righteous life that God desires."[6] Listen first, consider what you're going to say, and control your emotions.

- "Do not let any unwholesome talk come out of your mouths, but only what is helpful for building others up according to their needs, that it may benefit those who listen."[7] If you make an effort to take every thought captive to Christ, the words you speak should naturally be edifying to others.

- "Above all else, guard your heart [the central core of your beliefs], for it is the wellspring of life."[8] Whatever you believe in your heart, good or bad, will spring up in your thoughts and actions.

Shortly after I lost my carry-on and my cell phone, another trial came my way when my radio show was canceled and the expense allowance for my book tour was cut. I was very discouraged the morning I heard the news, but I put into practice the lessons I was learning about taking every thought captive to Christ. When I rehearsed God's promises and reminded myself of his faithfulness, I found that joy took root in my heart despite the circumstances. Later that same day, someone called me to talk about a whole new set of ministry opportunities, and I was able to thank God for opening up some exciting new doors.

Here's a very important point: Whether or not I received

another offer did not determine my joy. Rather it was God at work in my heart. The lesson I learned is this: When you suffer—while you're suffering—thank God for what he is refining in your character, and joy will soon follow. Trust God, and wait for him to show you his better plan. "Trust in the LORD with all your heart and lean not on your own understanding; in all your ways acknowledge him, and he will make your paths straight."[9]

How we think about our trials will determine our outlook on life. If we are griping, complaining, worried, or anxious all the time, our mood reveals what we really believe to be true about God and ourselves. On the other hand, if we set our minds on what is true, noble, right, pure, lovely, admirable, excellent, and praiseworthy, we won't be griping, complaining, worried, and anxious all the time. Instead, we will surrender our negative thoughts to the lordship of Christ and take on the mind of Christ, which is full of joy and peace.

When we make it a point to renew our minds by meditating on God's Word, our hearts will be more closely aligned with God's heart, and our outlook will encourage others as they see the work of Christ in us.

> When we make it a point to renew our minds by meditating on God's Word, our hearts will be more closely aligned with God's heart.

When all is said and done, I want my life to reflect God's Spirit. That means I want the fruit of the Spirit—love, joy, peace, patience, kindness, goodness, faithfulness, gentleness, and self-control—to characterize my life.[10] "Since we live by the Spirit, let us keep in step with the Spirit."[11]

As my thoughts change, I find that God is transforming me more and more into his likeness. I no longer try to change my feelings or moods like I used to. Now I realize that the root of the problem is my thought life. If I want to see positive change, I must take my thoughts captive under the lordship of Christ. Then my feelings and my moods will just naturally follow along.

Freedom in Captivity

As I have learned to surrender my thought life to God, I have found that he allows me to teach and speak with greater effectiveness. When I spoke in Detroit in September 2004, I had a sense that I was preaching with a greater level of conviction and passion. After the message, a woman approached me and gave me a note that both encouraged and admonished me. She said that if I would accept my true status with Christ—forgiven, called, blessed, and anointed—I would preach with much more boldness and power. Something in her words resonated in my spirit and I believed her. Since then, I've noticed that the more I take my thoughts captive, the more of God's truth I exude to others. I have also felt a greater measure of faith to pray for others. I believe that God is making me bolder as my belief in him strengthens.

> If we will accept our true status with Christ, we will live with much more boldness and power, because our lives are caught up with his.

I also realized something very important: What the woman in Detroit said to me is true for *every* Christian. If we will accept our true status with Christ—that our lives are now "hidden with Christ in God"[12]—we will live with much more boldness and power, because our lives are caught up with his and all authority and power has been given to him.[13] That promise is available to you every bit as much as it is to me.

After my encounter with the woman in Detroit, God led me to meditate on Romans 8:5-18 and Romans 13. These are powerful summaries of our need for God's Holy Spirit and the reality of what God is doing in us because of his Spirit. Not long after that, I was talking to a precious couple who were considering divorce. After I listened to their story for a while, I asked the wife, "Are you more concerned about the change that is needed in your life or the changes you think your husband needs?" She burst into tears, placed her head on the table, and sobbed. When she looked up, she said, "You're right. I've been blaming my husband for all my moods, and I can't take it anymore. I now understand and believe that I control my moods by my own beliefs and thoughts." She turned to her husband and said, "Honey, I will never again accuse you of being my source of misery. Starting today, I'm going to work on myself, with God's power, to become the wife you've always needed." By now, all three of us were in tears as we saw the Spirit of God change this woman's heart as she took responsibility for changing her thoughts. I used to be timid when counseling someone in a serious situation like this, but not anymore.

> Fear is an emotion and a lie from the enemy.

The next morning, I prayed for a woman to be set free from her fears and given total rest for her soul. That's when a new insight came to mind: *Fear is an emotion and a lie from the enemy.* "God has not given us a spirit of fear, but of power and of love and of a sound mind."[14] Fear causes us to believe that we cannot overcome our trials and that they are all bad for us. But if we know the *truth*, it will set us free.[15]

Fear is a reminder that we are meditating on negative thoughts or beliefs. Paul tells us to "set [our] minds on things above, not on earthly things."[16] He reminds us that we have died to ourselves and our lives now belong to Christ. We put to death our earthly nature by seeking and focusing on the things above where Christ dwells, and we are set free by his Spirit within us.

As I've learned to take every thought captive, I've noticed a new freedom in old areas of temptation. The other day, I was at a place where many young, beautiful women were wearing summer clothing: low-cut tops, swimsuits, and shorts. I tried for a while to simply look away, but no matter where I looked, there was another young, beautiful woman. Even at my age, I recognize their beauty, but I didn't allow my thoughts to go further than that. I've met a lot of men who would say, "It's impossible not to notice a woman or fantasize about her sexually. That's just the way men are wired." But how we're wired doesn't mean we can't take every thought captive to Christ. Job, a man who feared God, knew the power of lust and resisted it. He said, "I made a covenant with my eyes not to look lustfully at a girl."[17] Job, a man of integrity, knew that the Lord was aware of his every step.

I'm so thankful that God can keep my mind pure if I allow him to rule my thoughts. I can admire God's creation without resorting to sin. The same is true when I see new cars, trucks, fishing equipment, clothes, houses—you name it. Anything I desire can turn to lust if I allow my mind to wander from God's boundaries. But anything I desire can also be brought into submission to the will of God as I take every thought captive.

Here's a powerful prayer I use when I can't seem to stop my mind from wandering toward sin. I cry out to God and imagine myself as a little newborn baby, completely helpless and dependent. I tell God, "I can't take every thought captive on my own. I'm helpless and completely dependent on you. Please fortify me now." About

95 percent of the time, I find that my errant thoughts are brought under control.

You, too, can ask God to take control of your thoughts and beliefs, and when you do, you'll be able to control your mood swings, your words, and ultimately your actions. For out of your heart (which is closely connected to your mind and your will) flow the springs of life.[18]

YOUR RELATIONSHIP WITH GOD

1. Think about a particular sin you struggle with. How does your thought life contribute to the sin?

2. In your own words, what do you think it means to take every thought captive?

3. How is your thought life helping or hindering your relationship with God?

KEY VERSES: Romans 12:1-3; 2 Corinthians 10:5; Colossians 3:2; 1 Peter 1:13-16
Ask the Lord to help you renew your mind daily so that you can live a holy life, as he has called you to do.

MAKING IT PERSONAL
Take time to prayerfully consider what hinders the renewing of your mind. Perhaps it is a certain TV show, a magazine, or another form of entertainment. Make a point to replace it with something that helps you to set your mind on things above.

5

ACCEPTING GOD'S FILTER
FOR YOUR LIFE

At times it seems as if computers rule the world. In a sense, they are godlike in our culture. They seem all-powerful, all-knowing, and ever present. However, it doesn't take much experience to realize they are not all that powerful and they are fallible. They can be such a great help when they work, but they can also be a major headache. Have you ever wanted to just toss your computer out the window?

I didn't grow up around computers. My generation has had to learn to live with the fact that computers are here to stay. Somehow, I've survived several computer crashes. Back in the earlier days of my ministry, our office didn't have all the new technology that protects us now—the slightest technical glitch could set us back for days. We've come a long way since then.

Technological advances have created safety filters that protect and monitor the passing of information between computers. If we have the proper software installed, we are protected from viruses, spam, and other potential mishaps that can damage our data. With proper protection, all the information available online through the Internet and e-mails can't harm my computer the way it could have years ago.

Have you ever stopped to think about how God's sovereignty functions as a safety filter for our lives? If a simple software program can protect our computers from external attacks, how much more can God's eternal power block events in our lives that he doesn't want to let in?

Though most computer virus–protection software is reliable, it constantly needs to be updated, and it isn't infallible. God, of course, knows everything about us and our enemies; he is fully aware of our circumstances, and he knows what's coming. Furthermore, he is in-fallible, and his filter is set to conform us to his likeness.

I guess you could say that I have more confidence in my computer today than I did in the past, but I still know that technology cannot solve all my problems. My history with them attests to that! But my history with God gives me confidence that he will finish the good work he has started in me, and nothing can thwart his plans.[1] With my confidence in God's faithfulness, I now realize that my life is under control. I know that he has filtered everything that is going to happen to me today.

> My history with God gives me confidence that he will finish the good work he has started in me, and nothing can thwart his plans.

When I was in my blackest period, I was stressed out by unexpected occurrences. I struggled, thinking that a setback here or a delay there could actually thwart God's plan for me. Fear of failure was a huge source of stress for me. Finally, I figured out that there were many things out of my control, and there was nothing I could do about them. When I gave those concerns over to God, I experienced tremendous relief.

I remember how, early in my Christian life, the passages in the Bible on faith—such as Mark 11:22-24 and Luke 11 and 18—really inspired me. Christianity was fresh, new, and exciting to me, and I wanted to please Jesus with all my heart. My heart was filled with joy, and I wanted others to have it too. But through the years, I forgot that he had a plan for me, and I tried to come up with my own plan for my life.

Most of us want to know what God's will is for our lives. We want to know that we have purpose and that our lives matter. As Christians, we know that God is in control, no matter how out of control our lives may feel. But we often forget that God really is sovereign, and his sovereignty acts as a filter for our lives.

God's Filter Points Me to His Purposes

Maybe you are asking yourself, "What is God's purpose for me?" To answer this question, we must first consider the basic question of why we are here. When Jesus was asked to name the greatest commandment, he replied, "'Love the Lord your God with all your heart and with all your soul and with all your mind and with all your strength.' The second is this: 'Love your neighbor as yourself.' There is no commandment greater than these."[2] Jesus makes it clear that all of Scripture is summed up in these two commandments: Love God, and love your neighbor as yourself. Therefore, we can conclude that our purpose as human beings is rooted in relationships: loving God, loving ourselves, and loving others.[3]

> Our purpose as human beings is rooted in relationships: loving God, loving ourselves, and loving others.

Based on the words of Jesus, we know that God's ultimate purpose for us is rooted in loving relationships, but is there more? What about all the decisions we have to make in life—does God's will extend to our specific circumstances? Yes. I believe that each person has something unique to accomplish for the Lord. God's filter is set in such a way that we can discover what he has specifically called us to do. In *Joy That Lasts*, I used a series of questions called the Five *M*'s to explain how I found God's specific will for my life. These questions have helped me to stay focused on what God wants for me as he has faithfully revealed his will to me over the years.[4]

- *Master:* Who am I living for?
- *Mission:* What does God want me to do (for him and for others)?
- *Method:* How will I fulfill my mission?
- *Maintenance:* How will I evaluate and adjust my methods?
- *Mate:* Do my spouse and I agree about our mission and methods?

MASTER: WHO AM I LIVING FOR? The first *M* asks if our priorities are right before God. When my life got off track, it was because I had stopped asking this question and had begun to live for my own comfort, pleasure, and agenda. I've since learned that I must ask these questions every day: Who am I living for? and What is the evidence of that? Daily we must examine our hearts and our motives to make sure we are surrendering ourselves to the lordship of Christ. Here is an example of what I pray each morning: "God, I love you. I recommit my life to you today 100 percent. I understand that my most important calling is to love you and to love others as I love myself. I am committed to doing that, no matter what it takes."

MISSION: WHAT DOES GOD WANT ME TO DO (FOR HIM AND FOR OTHERS)? I know that serving other people with love is God's highest calling for me. I know that by loving and serving other people I am loving and serving God. Sometimes we serve others for selfish motives, but when we commit our efforts in prayer, we are more inclined to serve in response to God's love for us, not to gain reward or accolades from others.

When I first started in my ministry, I felt a tremendous burden to help people restore their broken relationships. Then several people in my church came to me and confirmed what God had laid on my heart. Years ago, when I was prayerfully asking God to reveal how I could best serve him, he used a man named Jim Stewart to confirm the direction I should take. Jim told me that God had stirred his heart to give financially to my mission. This seed money helped to launch my marriage seminars. After hearing further confirmation from friends, family, and other pastors and after waiting for God's peace to settle in my heart, I became convinced that I should go into this ministry full-time to help heal relationships.

Sometimes, the answers we are looking for from God don't come as quickly as we would like. It took me about two years to fully discern the steps that God wanted me to take to start my ministry. I've learned, however, that when we continue to put God first, he is always faithful to lead us toward his will for our lives. The time he gives us is a gift, and he does not intend for us to waste it. No time spent pursuing God's will in our lives is ever wasted.

> Sometimes, the answers we are looking for from God don't come as quickly as we would like.

METHOD: HOW WILL I FULFILL MY MISSION? God has gifted each person with a set of skills, knowledge, and life experiences. These unique combinations of assets help us to discern more specifically how we can serve God. I think it is important to realize that our calling may not be completely wrapped up in our occupations. What we "do for a living" may be a part of how we serve, but we are so much more than our jobs.

For most of my career, I have helped other people heal their relationships. God has allowed me to serve others through the books, media resources, and seminars I've produced over the years. However, my time off the job is just as important to God. He is concerned with how I spend every moment of my life. How I serve my family and friends is also a part of the mission God has for me. Regardless of where you are, whether at work, at home, or at play, take note of the people that God has placed in your path. How can you better love your neighbor as yourself?

Take note of the people that has God placed in your path. How can you better love your neighbor as yourself?

What a great realization it is to know that God has created—in advance—a great plan for our lives.[5] I love waking up in the morning and telling my best friend, "Lord, maybe today is the day you'll open the door to one of the dreams you have put on my heart. I can hardly wait to see what you have planned for my day."

MAINTENANCE: HOW WILL I EVALUATE AND ADJUST MY METHODS? Sometimes God gives us a vision for what he wants us to accomplish, but he doesn't give us a step-by-step plan. Often, we don't know what is going to work until we test some different methods. I've tried all kinds of things in my service to God. Some have succeeded beyond my wildest dreams, and others haven't worked at all. Some of my most crushing defeats have come when what seemed to be great ideas just didn't pan out. But I've learned to adjust my methods and keep trying.

I've already told the story of how a direct-to-church campaign and a national media campaign in support of my books and seminars didn't work out, even though they seemed like good ideas at the time. God used those efforts to refine my character rather than to launch a successful new ministry. But now I have other opportunities that I'm evaluating and other methods I'm considering. The point is that we must remain clear on the purpose, which is serving God and other people according to the gifts and opportunities that God has supplied—and flexible on the methods. What works today may not be the best choice tomorrow. It is easy to rely on what is most familiar and miss ways to improve our effectiveness. If the method becomes our primary focus, we can end up missing our whole mission. Evaluating and adjusting our methods takes thoughtful, prayerful discipline, but it is worth the effort to keep us on track toward God's purpose for our lives.

> I've learned to adjust my methods and keep trying.

MATE: DO MY PARTNER AND I AGREE ABOUT OUR MISSION AND METHODS? If you're not married, this next point can apply to you and a ministry partner. However, it is absolutely essential for married folks to get this one right. My life has been successful only when I have been in total harmony with my wife on the mission and the methods I have pursued. There have been times when I thought that Norma just didn't see what God was leading me to do. I've gone ahead with plans, even though I felt uneasy about them because I knew she didn't agree, but I can't remember a time when God blessed what I was doing if Norma was in disagreement. Today, I won't move in a direction unless she and I are in harmony. This simple principle has saved my neck time and again.

When I decided a few years ago that God wanted me to retire and turn my ministry over to my sons, I initially didn't include my wife in those plans (I know—dumb). Norma reacted strongly against my decision, and all her expressed fears were realized when I didn't heed her warnings and her counsel. It turned out not to be the right decision for us. God gives us partners in marriage to balance us out; often they are able to see things that we can't see on our own.

> God may call a husband and a wife to different specific missions, but he still wants them to consult with each other.

God may call a husband and a wife to different specific missions (different ways of loving and serving others), but he still wants them to consult with each other. This may seem like an obvious point, but we can quickly forget our obligation to our spouse. Part of becoming "one flesh" is putting the needs of your mate above your own. Ask yourself, "How will this decision affect my marriage? What will this mean to my spouse?" Your spouse is a filter that God uses to guide you. Your oneness in marriage will be a great asset in finding God's specific direction for your life.

God's Filter Is Always On

God is at work in every aspect of life. He knows what is going to happen now and throughout eternity. I take great comfort in God's sovereignty. No matter what I might experience that I don't understand, I know that God is working it out for my ultimate good and for the good of others. I give him complete control.

I know that God can block anything from coming my way. Likewise, he can allow anything he wants to come my way. He is all-powerful. So now when I find myself in a dilemma, I view it differently. I know that God is ultimately in control, and he has allowed this experience to occur. No matter what, he can take anything negative and turn it into something positive in my life. I'm not always able to accept this fact as quickly as I'd like, but I do trust God's filter for my life.

"Give thanks in all circumstances, for this is God's will for you in Christ Jesus."[6] Sure, I knew this verse years ago. But I had forgotten how to be grateful for all that was happening to me. I now take refuge in Romans 8:28: "We know that in all things God works for the good of those who love him, who have been called according to his purpose."

We live in a fallen world, and bad things are going to happen to all of us. But the great news is that God takes all our experiences and uses them for our good in our lives. God can cause even the most undesirable circumstance to work for our good. He knows everything about this world and everything about you and me. He even knows when a lone sparrow falls. If he takes time to care for the sparrows, I know how much more he watches over me. He always uses the bad things that happen to us to conform us closer to his likeness. It may take us a while to see it, but the fruit of our lives will attest to God's work in us.

> It may take us a while to see it, but the fruit of our lives will attest to God's work in us.

Speaking of sparrows, something rather unpleasant but humorous happened just after this renewal started in my life. It was maybe two weeks after my kidney transplant, and I was able to walk only short distances. I was still in Los Angeles with my wife and my daughter. Norma had gone shopping or to run an errand, and Kari and I were sitting in the hotel room. I said, "I'd like to take a walk outside."

Prior to my release from the hospital, the doctors and nurses had told me, "There are certain things that cannot happen to you over the next six to ten weeks. Number one, you cannot under any circumstances touch bird droppings." Norma and I have chickens at home, but I was instructed not to pick them up or touch any of their droppings because the droppings are highly toxic to kidney transplant patients. Over and over, the doctors firmly instructed me, "Whatever you do, do not touch the droppings of any animal. No dogs, cats, birds, whatever." They emphasized this repeatedly.

"OK, I got it. No animal droppings."

On this particular day—a gorgeous, warm, sunny November day—Kari and I started our stroll outside the hotel in downtown Los Angeles. I hadn't walked more than twenty feet from the hotel door before I felt a large, watery drop on my head. I thought, *What was that? Is there a sprinkler on? Did somebody spit from the building and hit me?* As I looked up, I put my hand on my head and quickly realized that my hair and my hand were full of gooey, black-and-white bird droppings. I don't think it was a sparrow. It was probably a pigeon, but judging by the size of the "bomb," I would have said it was an eagle or a California condor. The whole side of my head was wet. The goop was running into my ear and down the side of my face. At first, I panicked, afraid it would get into my eyes. I turned around to see if any water was nearby. I spotted a fountain, but as I started to scoop up a handful of water, I could see the green scum on the sides of the basin. More germs! I just started laughing.

The first thing that came to mind was that something like this had never happened to me before—and thankfully it has never happened since! *Why now,* I thought, *when I am the most susceptible to a disease that is carried through bird droppings?* But then I realized that God could have controlled this. I could have taken two more steps in front of the bird or been two steps slower coming out of the hotel. But no, I was right where I needed to be for the full load to drop squarely on my head. I just laughed and said, "God, you must have a great sense of humor." Strange as it may sound, I saw this as a bonding experience with the Lord. When I turned around to Kari, she was bent over double, laughing her head off.

My hair and my hand were full of gooey, black-and-white bird droppings.

In the past, I would have said, "Stop laughing; this isn't funny. I could be dead tomorrow because of this." After we regained our composure, we went back upstairs. I took two showers and washed my hair twice with antiseptic shampoo. By God's grace, I was not adversely affected by the incident. And by his grace, I was able to laugh about it and learn from it.

I later spent time in my hotel room looking up verses about how God ordains our steps. First Peter 1:3-7 reminded me that God refines our faith like gold through all the trials we encounter. James tells us to "consider it pure joy, my brothers, whenever you face trials of many kinds, because you know that the testing of your faith develops perseverance. Perseverance must finish its work so that you may be mature and complete, not lacking anything."[7] What a great promise! If we will persevere, we will not lack anything. Therefore, we can give thanks and not be embittered by the things that happen to us.

We can give thanks and not be embittered by the things that happen to us.

Sometime later, I talked to Kari when she was having a

particularly stressful day. She had been late to a weekly class that was very important to her daughter. Kari felt stressed because she wanted to make sure her daughter benefited as much as possible from the sessions, but now they had lost fifteen minutes of training by being late. After the session, they presented Kari with the bill, and she found out that she owed a lot more money for the training than she thought.

On top of that, she was having difficulty with her eldest son's fourth-grade teacher, who assigned a level of homework that seemed better suited for a college class. Kari knew that her son had a lot of pressure on him, and she was turning the situation over in her mind, trying to figure it all out.

I could hear the stress in her voice over the phone, and I knew that all of these concerns were directly related to her expectations, which were actually quite normal. I reminded her that God knew all about her day. Now I wasn't saying that she was supposed to be late or that God had told my grandson's teacher to overwhelm him with homework. Rather, I wanted Kari to remember that God could take all these bad experiences and use them for good in her family's life. She wasn't seeing them as filtered by God, under his sovereign care.

> I wanted her to remember that God could take all these bad experiences and use them for good.

Later that evening, I went over and helped my grandson with some of his math problems. I minored in math in college, so I figured I could handle it at the fourth-grade level—and I could have if they hadn't changed all the terminology! I offered to stay for a while so that Kari and her husband, Roger, could have some time together to pray. Finally, I asked Kari, "Did God know all that would happen today? Did anything escape his notice? Did God know ahead of time what the bill was going to be and what the teacher was going to say? Did God allow all these things to happen?"

She dropped her head a little bit and said, "Yes. Because God could have chosen to filter out all those things from my life."

The next morning, Kari called me first thing and said, "Dad, I prayed last night and went through my expectations. I was not seeing that God allowed my set of circumstances and that these struggles could be used in my life for God's glory and for the good of my children. Thank you for reminding me.

"By the way," she added, "I am doing much better today. I am looking at everything that happens as allowed by God."

As Christians, we know that we live in a fallen world, and things happen to us that we cannot explain. We know rain falls on the just and the unjust.[8] Though God is not the source of our problems, he does allow certain things to happen. Does that mean we can carelessly walk out in front of a speeding car without being hurt? No. Does it mean, "Life is life, and nobody can do anything about it"? Well, I do tend to have that attitude at times about the things in life that are out of my control. But for the things in life that I can control—my thinking, my actions, my love for people, my expectations—I want to take responsibility. God does empower us to exercise self-control.

> As Christians, we know that we live in a fallen world, and things happen to us that we cannot explain.

Of everyone in the human race, over whom do I have the most control? That's right—myself. I can influence other people. I can try to motivate them or encourage them. I can do a number of things to try to help them, but I cannot change them. I can change only myself. Because I can't change other people, I choose to work on changing myself and leave the rest to God. I especially work on my thoughts and beliefs, because I know that I will become what I think about and believe.

When things hit that are beyond my control, there is nothing I can do about it except acknowledge God's sovereignty. At the airport the other day, I was randomly selected to have all my luggage inspected. As the security people dug through everything, I just said, "God, you could have picked someone else. I don't mind spending time to make sure that air travel is safe. It looks like I might miss my flight. But even if I do, God, you are in charge of my time. I can go to Plan B, Plan C, or Plan D, if necessary." Oh, how freeing it is to relax and allow God's filter to refine my life and my faith. Meanwhile, my stress levels remain low.

> How freeing it is to relax and allow God's filter to refine my life and my faith.

Job understood that God is in control. At the beginning of his story, we learn that Satan is roaming about the earth looking for his next victim. He wants to test Job, and the Lord allows it.[9] In fact, God even prompts the devil to consider this blameless servant. Satan is given permission to afflict Job, but God still has the enemy on a leash. His powers are limited. Job's family is attacked physically and spiritually, his house collapses, his servants and livestock are burned, and he is afflicted with painful sores from the soles of his feet to the top of his head, yet the story ends in a remarkable way. Job remains faithful to God through his pain and suffering, and he is made prosperous again. The Lord gives Job twice as much as he had before. Job then declares to the Lord, "I know that you can do all things; no plan of yours can be thwarted. You asked, 'Who is this that obscures my counsel without knowledge?' Surely I spoke of things I did not understand, things too wonderful for me to know."[10]

This story is a great illustration of God's sovereign filter at work in our lives. Though the enemy plots against us, we are still safe in the arms of the Lord. I think Satan learned a few things through the testing of Job. Not only did he lose the battle for this humble servant's soul, but Job's love for God was made stronger through all the adversity. Job learned to trust God more deeply in the darkest of places. What a legacy he left for his family!

I've shared with you some examples from my life that in the past would have caused me to really struggle. Take a moment now and review the Five *M*'s in light of your own life.

- Who are you living for?
- What does God want you to do (for him and for others)?
- How will you fulfill your mission?
- How will you evaluate and adjust your methods?
- If you're married, do you and your spouse agree about your mission and methods?

Think about the events in your life this week. Does anything need to change in order for you to accept God's filter for your life? Are you trusting that God is ultimately in control? Do you realize that he really is on your side? Do you recognize that God's filter is set specifically to help you bear fruit in your life because he wants you to be the best servant for him and others? God does not take away our ability to make choices. Sometimes, our own decisions will cause us heartache and grief. He can use even our worst decisions to shape and refine our character and make us more like him. The God whom we serve is the Creator and Master of all things. He is free to do whatever he wills. We can take comfort in knowing that he is not subject to our whims and weaknesses and that he makes his decisions based on his unconditional and everlasting love for us.

YOUR RELATIONSHIP WITH GOD

1. Think about your relationship with God right now. Who is more in control of your life, you or God? Explain.

2. Recall a time in your life that was particularly difficult. How are you able to see God's hand in the situation now? What can you see about yourself that you couldn't see when you were in the midst of the trial?

3. How do we balance God's sovereignty with our free will? Should we accept all circumstances in our lives as God's filter? Why or why not?

KEY VERSES: Romans 8:28-32
Meditate on God's careful watch over your life and thank him for knowing all the details of your day.

MAKING IT PERSONAL
Write down something in your life that you know you cannot resolve without God's help. List what you can do to move toward resolution, and list what only God can do. Pray about this issue for the next thirty days, and see how the Lord uses your free will and his loving filter to work on your behalf.

6

WORSHIPING GOD
IN THE MIDST OF TRIALS

Nothing in life should be able to shake our joy in the Lord. Nothing in life should interrupt our worship of him. No matter what trials we face, we can still worship God and be thankful. A grateful heart is a healthy heart. God can always use what hurts us to teach us where we need to grow. Instead of fighting God when life stings us, we can learn to use our trials as opportunities to trust God like never before. We all know what it means to feel the *expected* and *unexpected* blows that life can bring. Trials. Struggles. Problems. Uncomfortable encounters. Irritations. But regardless of our circumstances, there is much good to be found if we will open our eyes to what God is doing.

In this chapter, I want to take you through an exercise that will teach you how to turn a negative in your life into a positive. You'll see that it is possible to believe and think rightly even in the midst of great pain.

One of my favorite authors, M. Scott Peck, begins his signature book, *The Road Less Traveled*, with this classic statement: "Life is difficult. . . . Once we truly know that life is difficult—once we truly understand and accept it—then life is no longer difficult. Because once it is accepted, the fact that life is difficult no longer matters."[1] After enduring my share of trials, big and small, I've learned to embrace them with gratitude. I know it sounds odd, but I have learned to embrace adversity with the joy of the Lord. Jesus calls us to adopt such radical thinking and to live out the ways of his kingdom here on earth. If we follow him, we will suffer hardship, but we will also gain our heavenly reward. Jesus said, "All men will hate you because of me. . . . [But] by standing firm you will gain life."[2] Here's the bottom line: We can't stop trials, so instead we should choose to get as much good from them as we can. I now see my trials as faithful friends that point me to God and conform me into his image.

> Nothing in life should be able to shake our joy in the Lord. Nothing in life should interrupt our worship of him.

It has been a blessing to finally learn how to let God use hardship and suffering to refine me. I knew this was a truth taught in Scripture (James 1:2-4; 1 Peter 1:6-7; 4:12-14), but I have only recently learned how to really apply it in my life. Here is my paraphrase of James 1:2-4: "Consider the joy that you gain, my brothers, whenever you face trials and testing, because you know that the hot fires of life purify your faith while developing perseverance in you. Let the trials continue until you have been made complete, lacking in nothing." From God's point of view, "not lacking in anything" refers to spiritual maturity and wisdom, which God desires for us all to attain with his power. As I have begun to worship God through my trials, I have learned what it means to be an overcomer—victorious through even the worst of days.

After learning many spiritual lessons the hard way, I finally learned to stand on God's Word: "And my God will meet all your needs according to his glorious riches in Christ Jesus."[3] His Word is powerful and gives us the faith we need to believe that God is working out everything according to his riches and our needs. That is a powerful promise! It is amazing to me how much peace is available to us through the most devastating trial if we trust God to take care of us. He wants you to share every trial with him, every struggle.

When my kidneys started to fail, I wasn't interested in what God wanted for my life. My only concern was with getting healed, not with anything that God might want to teach me about trusting him. The whole ordeal of undergoing surgery was not at all what I had in mind. Looking back, however, I'm so grateful to God that he did not heal me instantly. I needed to learn the hard way about the gift of life. I needed to suffer through a serious trial so that I would have the opportunity to be confronted with the depravity of my soul. Yes, God wanted me to be healed; but more important than my kidneys, he wanted to heal my heart and my soul. He wanted to give me a chance to reexamine my life. I thank God that he allowed me to persevere through my surgery and recovery. Kidney failure turned out to be the best thing that ever happened to me.

Treasure Hunting Our Trials

After years of fussing and fuming in the face of adversity, I have finally recognized that trials and testing are God's precious jewels thrown in my path. Finding the good in bad circumstances has become like a treasure hunt to me. If you've ever seen a pirate movie, you know that treasure hunting can be perilous, life threatening, and full of action. An experienced treasure hunter knows that there's a cost involved, and it might even mean losing his life; but the treasure is worth it, because it is precious and valuable. Sometimes, treasure is buried in the most unexpected places.

The same is true when we treasure hunt with God. Who would naturally think to look for treasure in the midst of adversity? Not me. But I have discovered some of the most precious gems in my life during some of the darkest times. I just needed to learn how to uncover them. Treasure hunting with God involves an investment of my heart and my will. I must choose to trust him, even when I can't see what he's doing—which is often the case. When I accept the fact that God is sovereign and he knows what is best for me, I then begin to discover the treasure he has cultivated in me like a precious pearl.

Let me show you how to discover God's treasure in even the bleakest circumstances. Think for a moment about some of your worst experiences. Maybe you have endured a broken relationship with a parent, a child, or a spouse. Or perhaps your trial is as painful as sexual abuse as a child. Maybe you have recently been fired from a job. Or perhaps you're the victim of an auto accident that was not your fault but left you with physical disabilities. Whatever source of pain you carry, God wants to use it as an instrument of good in your life. I know it's difficult to understand, but God uses suffering in our lives to accomplish his ultimate purpose: to form us into the likeness of Christ. Even Jesus, God's only begotten Son, suffered in order to accomplish God's purpose: "Although he was a son, he learned obedience from what he suffered

> When we commit ourselves, by an act of the will and an investment of the heart, to worship God in all circumstances, our lives can't help but be enriched.

and, once made perfect, he became the source of eternal salvation for all who obey him."[4]

When we commit ourselves, by an act of the will and an investment of the heart, to worship God in all circumstances, our lives can't help but be enriched. Sure, it's normal to avoid pain. No one really wants to go through trials. But we know that "life is difficult," and trials are something that God promises will come our way. They are unavoidable. Because it is more a matter of *when* trials will come, not *if*, we need a godly perspective for how to view our trials.

I am convinced that Romans 8:28 is always true: "We know that in all things God works for the good of those who love him, who have been called according to his purpose." It doesn't matter who we are or what difficulty we are facing, God always has a way of working out everything for our good and his glory. We can make a complete mess of things, or others can mess things up for us, but God is always at work on our behalf. Have you ever stopped to realize that there is a treasure in every trial?

> God's refining process can take an embittered, cold heart and transform it into a heart of gold.

Treasure hunting for a Christian is a lot like turning lead into gold. God's refining process can take an embittered, cold heart and transform it into a heart of gold. It is easy to forget what God promises when we persevere through trials—maturity, wisdom, joy, faith, glory, and honor. "Blessed is the man who perseveres under trial, because when he has stood the test, he will receive the crown of life that God has promised to those who love him" (James 1:12). We must see our suffering as God sees it—as a refining fire that purifies us and makes us more like Christ.

Are you ready to do some treasure hunting? Here's how the process works:

Write down at least one difficult trial that you have faced. Write down as many trials as come to mind, but you may want to treasure hunt with one trial at a time so you won't be overwhelmed. If you have never done an exercise like this, you may not want to start with a current trial, because you may still be in the grief stage. If so, please allow time to pass without trying to stop the pain. Let the painful emotions emerge within all of your trials. Don't deny the pain, don't wish or hope that it will soon leave, and don't try to shorten the pain. James makes the point very clear: "Perseverance must finish its work so that you may be mature and complete, not lacking anything."[5] Let the pain continue until you are transformed, which will only happen when God has completed his work in you.

Write down the benefits of each trial. Focus on the positive and write down everything that comes to mind. What have you learned? How have you grown? How have you seen the fruit of the Spirit and other positive character traits formed through your trials? Depending on the severity and type of the trial, you may find this step very difficult, but stay with it. You may also want to ask a group of friends or family members in whom you can confide to help you with this exercise.

Here is a list of potential benefits that can come from any painful trial. Feel free to circle some that you recognize in yourself:

patience . . . understanding . . . empathy . . . caring
. . . compassion . . . gentleness . . . tenderness . . .
understanding . . . forthrightness . . . boldness . . .
energy . . . humility . . . meekness . . . forgiveness
. . . perseverance . . . hope . . . mercy . . . love . . .

joy . . . grace . . . peace . . . kindness . . .
goodness . . . self-control . . . wisdom . . . purity . . .
holiness . . .

When your list of benefits is complete, start another list and write down your strengths, things you appreciate about yourself. Write down what you like about your personality, talents, physical characteristics, mental or spiritual attributes, and so on. This will help you to develop a spirit of thanksgiving toward God instead of a spirit of resentment or bitterness. Every problem—great or small—has some sort of treasure in it waiting to be discovered.

> Every problem—great or small—has some sort of treasure in it waiting to be discovered.

These two lists—how you've benefited from trials, and what you already deeply appreciate about yourself—will now serve as reminders of how valuable you are to God, to others, and to yourself. God loves you so much that he will make all things work together for good as you continue to love him, yourself, and others. One of the most amazing mysteries about our imperfect lives is that God uses our trials, setbacks, and difficulties to mold us into his image.

Gather one or more supportive friends to help you treasure hunt your biggest trials. We all have blind spots and need the counsel of others in order to get a more accurate view of ourselves—especially if we have faced difficult trials. Sometimes we have trouble seeing the good, but others can see the good *in us.* Ask people who can be objective and see things about you that you cannot see. For me, my children and their spouses are particularly helpful.

Use your list of positive traits to love others in very practical ways. This will complete the positive cycle. Loving others as Christ has loved us is our ultimate purpose in life. As you invest more in others, you will sense great fulfillment and purpose. Take a few minutes and list the best ways that others could serve you. What would you really like others to do for you, to say to you, or to be for you? Now go and do likewise.

Praise in the Midst of Pain

Reflecting on my own life, I can think of many painful trials over the past thirty years. My list looks something like this:

- Losing one of my grandsons before he was born
- Losing my TV infomercial because of a controversy surrounding the celebrity hosts
- Traveling on commercial airlines (When you travel as much as I do, this can be a real trial.)
- Any extended disharmony with my wife or family
- Almost drowning in Mexico
- Almost dying from a heart attack
- The weeks before and after my kidney transplant
- Losing my life plan for ministry in 2004

When the direct-to-church campaign for my books and seminars fell apart in 2004, it was a significant but temporary setback. But when the subsequent media marketing campaign collapsed and I lost what felt like everything in the span of a week, it was devastating. For about three months, I was not in a frame of mind to treasure hunt this trial. But even though I was grieving over my failed plan, I made a conscious effort (engaging both my will and my heart) to offer praise and thanksgiving to God. Sometimes my prayers sounded like this:

God, h-e-l-l-l-l-l-p! I'm drowning here. But I choose to give you thanks for this tremendous trial. I can't wait until the pain subsides and you allow me to see some of what you are doing for my good and your glory. I trust you. And even though I'm in the midst of the storm and it hurts—it hurts really bad—I thank you that you are in control and that you are in the midst of the storm with me.

I tried to envision the person I would become if I surrendered my will fully to God. I knew he was working everything out for my good, even though it didn't feel very good at the time. It is important for me to say that throughout this painful period, I cried out to God in prayer every day. I stayed connected, even though for a long time, my emotional pain, my feelings of failure, and my hopelessness were all I had to offer him.

> I knew that God was working everything out for my good, even though it didn't feel very good at the time.

After a while, I began meeting with my staff to figure out a new direction for our ministry. I continued doing my monthly seminars, and I kept looking for opportunities to tell others about the new message that God had laid on my heart that could help couples. But I honestly did not know what direction to go in the future.

I survived the fall of 2004, and the weeks dragged on without much change. But I continued to seek God for direction, and I trusted that he was refining my character to make it more like his, even though I couldn't see it. After about three months, my grief subsided, and I sensed that I was regaining my equilibrium. Still, the winter months dragged on, with no new ministry opportunities on the horizon. But I kept seeking God and thanking him, knowing that he really did have the best plan in mind for me.

First Signs of Blessing

Blessings can be hard to see in the midst of disappointment and pain. But God is faithful to give us the encouragement we need to keep looking. After what felt like a very long winter, spring finally came. Toward the end of March 2005, during one of my seminars in South Florida, one of my staff members talked with a staff member from Rick Warren's Purpose Driven Ministries. He invited us to discuss some potential projects. In May, I flew out to meet with these folks to consider ways in which we might partner with them to reach couples and enrich marriages all over the world. I had no doubt that God had orchestrated this meeting for me. Every conversation that weekend seemed to confirm that my ministry should head in this direction. On almost every point, it seemed that my prayer to reach pastors, develop mentors for small groups, and minister to couples was being expanded by a factor of ten. It was quite affirming to listen to their presentations and to see the potential for collaboration. It felt like a hug from God!

After that weekend, I asked myself, "Did God take me through the pain of 2004 to get me ready to enlarge my dreams tenfold?" I believe he did. As this book goes to press, we're still in developmental discussions with our potential ministry partner, but I'm optimistic about the future. Even if this particular partnership doesn't work out, I'm confident that God has something good in store for me. He will be faithful to turn everything negative into something for my good and his glory. Here are just a few of the benefits I have gained from the setbacks in my ministry:

- I am more empathetic toward pastors who are carrying a vision from God but feel alone and defeated by their church leaders.
- My patience has doubled for accomplishing my goals.

- I don't rely as much on other people's promises for my ministry, but I am more focused on God showing me his plan, his timing, and his way.
- I have let go of my feelings of angst toward vendors who can't deliver what they promise. I have seen God work things out in ways I could not have imagined.
- I realize I could lose the pending partnership opportunity, but my confidence is in God more than ever before, rather than in other people.
- God has granted me his supernatural peace far more than what I could have imagined.

When we learn the discipline of treasure hunting our trials, we will find that the best treasures are all things that will last, like our character and growing in our love for other people. When I stop and compare myself with what I was like last year or the year before, I'm absolutely amazed. Sometimes I regress, and it's as if I'm starting all over again with some qualities of my personality or character; but I'm increasingly aware that God is giving me his nature through the powerful work of the Holy Spirit in my life.

I hope that, like me, you find yourself looking at your current struggles in a new light, as a chance to grow in your worship of God. As unnatural as it feels at times, our trials really are an opportunity to express our gratitude to God. Worshiping God continually is our primary calling. We sometimes forget that worship and praise are not just for times of celebration. Worship is something that should be consciously pouring out of me at all times. When we worship God, our minds are lifted out of and above our circumstances. True worship says, "All I really need is the Lord in my life, because he will supply all my needs, and I am grateful." Every trial bears the seeds of God's goodness and love. Therefore, we can "give

thanks in all circumstances, for this is God's will for [us] in Christ
Jesus."[6]

YOUR RELATIONSHIP WITH GOD

1. What is the most difficult trial you have faced in your life? How has
   God used it to draw you closer to him and mature your faith?

2. When you are going through a trial, big or small, do you feel more
   connected to God, or less connected?

3. What have your trials taught you about God? About yourself?

KEY VERSES: Read James 1:1-16

MAKING IT PERSONAL
Think of some people you know who have a growing, healthy relationship
with God. Ask them how they endured a particularly difficult trial. What
can you learn from their testimonies that will enhance your relationship
with God?

7

SEEKING GODLY COUNSEL

I don't know about you, but I have made some really dumb decisions in my life. Most were pretty minor and thankfully didn't have any life-altering effects, but some were major mistakes that rocked my whole world, my family, and my ministry.

Have you ever noticed how many decisions you make in a day? In our consumer-oriented, "have it your way" culture, we have more opportunities to choose than ever before. And we have the freedom to decide most things on our own. We choose what we want to believe, and we do what seems right to us. But this individualistic perspective doesn't work very well for Christians. When we make decisions, we must consider what God wants as well as what is good for other people.

If we want to do the will of God so that we're becoming more like him day by day, we must include him in our decisions. You might think it sounds self-centered and egotistical to say that the God of the universe cares about every detail of our lives. But the Bible teaches that God has every hair on our heads numbered, and he is not only concerned about the details of our lives, but he also cares for every last sparrow and the flowers of the field.[1] He wants us to involve him in every detail of the day. We can depend on him for wisdom and direction. James writes, "If any of you lacks wisdom, he should ask God, who gives generously to all without finding fault, and it will be given to him."[2] This wisdom from heaven "is first of all pure; then peace-loving, considerate, submissive, full of mercy and good fruit, impartial and sincere."[3]

Godly Decisions Involve Godly Counsel

Early in my adult years, I discovered that my personality tended toward making snap decisions without even noticing the wisdom that God had placed within my reach. Many mentors and friends along the way could have saved me from making some horrible decisions, if only I would have taken advantage of their counsel. Proverbs 13:10 says, "Wisdom is found in those who take advice." Well, I haven't always practiced wise decision making. I learned the hard way. After making some of the dumbest decisions of my life in isolation, I finally learned to slow down and allow myself time to seek the counsel of God, my wife, and other advisors.

> I finally learned to slow down and allow myself time to seek the counsel of God, my wife, and other advisors.

I still don't know what possessed me in the mid-1990s to announce my retirement to my family and friends without ever consulting with anyone. Some of my close friends have suggested I was having some sort of identity crisis mixed with a season of burnout. I can remember feeling as if I had said everything about relationships that I had to say and feeling that I lacked vision for what to do next. I also felt some ambivalence about my financial success. My parents were both very simple and poor, and no one in my family had enjoyed much success by the world's standards. I think I felt a little bit guilty. I can also remember thinking that it made sense to retire while I was still young enough to enjoy it. But little did I realize the adverse effects my decision would have.

Not long after I made my hasty announcement, my health problems began. According to cellular biologist Dr. Bruce Lipton, the cells in our bodies literally react to our words, our thoughts, and our beliefs. No wonder the average American male dies sometime between three and four years after he announces his retirement. When a man says out loud, "I'm done, I'm finished with working, and now I can do what I want," his body concludes that it has done all that it needs to do and it's time to shut down. After what I have read over the past few years, I don't ever plan to retire! I may change occupations or ministries, but I'm available to be used by God for whatever purpose he desires, every day, for the rest of my life. I don't recall seeing anywhere in Scripture where God tells us to stop loving and serving others, which is our main mission in life. So what's to retire from?

> When a man says out loud, "I'm done, I'm finished with working, and now I can do what I want," his body concludes that it has done all that it needs to do and it's time to shut down.

Whatever the reasons for my decision, it certainly wasn't the result of prayer and seeking wise counsel from my family and godly friends. I've had the privilege of knowing such wise Christian leaders as Dr. James Dobson, Henry Blackaby, and Chuck Swindoll. I can just imagine Chuck's robust laughter if he had ever heard me say what I said to my family at the time: "I think I've done enough for God for one lifetime." What was I thinking? Though God had provided plenty of wise counsel for me to draw upon, I didn't utilize it. I still shudder to think how unwise I was.

What about you? Whatever your stage in life, you, too, have access to many wise counselors. Are you doing the same dumb thing that I did by avoiding the advice of pastors, teachers, friends, business leaders, and family members who love God? What important decision are you currently facing that you are afraid to share with others?

One night, when we lived in Phoenix, we invited all the couples on our advisory board to a meeting at a friend's house so I could present a new idea and strategy for our ministry. I spent hours preparing my notes, and on the way to the meeting, I asked Norma what she thought of my new strategy. My motive for asking her was to get encouragement and support just in case the meeting didn't go well. She reminded me that she had not heard the entire idea until that very moment. Then she paused and said nothing. I finally said to her impatiently, "Well, what do you think?" She looked at me with a concerned expression and said, "Gary, I don't think you would like to hear what I think right now!"

> **W**hat important decision are you currently facing that you are afraid to share with others?

Moments later, we pulled into our friend's driveway and opened the car doors. Others were pulling up and most of the men were asking me about the new strategy I was going to share. Once everyone was seated and refreshments had been served, the host welcomed everyone and led us in a very special time of prayer. When it was over, it was my turn to share my new strategy for our ministry. I spent the first few minutes telling a story about a speaking engagement where more than nine hundred men at a campground near Portland had responded to my message, and many of them asked me to speak more often to men. Up to that point, all my messages were focused on married couples. I read some powerful statistics on the needs of men in America. I finally shared my heart about changing our entire ministry focus to work with men only. The men in the room seemed very curious and asked me lots of good questions about things I hadn't thought of. I saw that as their support.

Then one man with whom I had done some marriage counseling asked a question that no one had yet raised. He got everyone's attention by yelling out loud, "Norma Smalley." Everyone got quiet. He said, "Norma Smalley, I want to know what you think of this idea after being involved in a couples ministry for more than ten years." Norma looked at me first to read my facial expression. I had a reputation with my family of looking stern if something inappropriate was about to be said.

The man repeated his question: "Norma . . . what do you think of this idea?"

Norma shared her perspective and began to cry. She explained very clearly how God had originally called us into a ministry focusing on the

"If God is blessing what you are presently doing, don't change course!"

needs of couples. She shared how fulfilling it had been to see God bless and enrich so many people through the hundreds of thousands of books that had been distributed through our monthly seminars, our letters, and so on.

When she was done, the man who had asked the question stood up and said, "Men and women, unless you think differently, I believe the decision is obvious, and I'll quote Dr. Howard

Hendricks: 'If God is blessing what you are presently doing, don't change course!'"

Everyone seemed excited that God had used Norma to speak sound advice, and they all began to leave. I was devastated. I couldn't get out to the car fast enough. On the ride home, I told Norma how incredibly hurt I was that she had ruined my new idea and strategy. There were tears streaking down my face as I thought about how much hope I had put into this dream, and now it was over.

One month later, I received a phone call from a football coach in Colorado who wanted my help to launch a citywide retreat for men in Boulder. His vision was to reach at least three thousand men in the Denver metro area. I told him it would be an honor, but when I got off the phone I was thinking, *Lord, I thought you wanted me to speak only to couples.*

To my surprise, when Norma heard about the invitation, she encouraged me to go. She said, "Gary, I believe our ministry is to couples, but speaking to husbands is critical to helping any marriage!"

In June 1991, I spoke to more than four thousand men at the University of Colorado basketball arena. Afterward, the organizers got together to discuss plans for the next year. They wanted to go statewide and use the Boulder football stadium to reach ten thousand men. I told them I would help them and that it should be advertised nationwide. That next year, I spoke again with other keynote speakers and pastors, and there were fifty thousand

> Because I know firsthand what happens when I make decisions in a vacuum apart from God, I now make a point to talk all day long with him about everything. He is involved in all my daily decisions.

men in attendance. After that successful gathering, my new friend, Coach Bill McCartney, left his nationally ranked college football team to devote his full-time attention to his blossoming men's ministry called Promise Keepers.

What had God been saying through my wife's good and wise counsel that night in Phoenix? He was saying, "Gary, I have not called you to organize a men's ministry but I will use you to be part of one that will be bigger than you could ever imagine."

Because I know firsthand what happens when I make decisions in a vacuum apart from God, I now make a point to talk all day long with him about everything. He is involved in all my daily decisions. I am fully dependent on his counsel and guidance. He speaks to me through his Word, through direct impressions in my spirit, and through the wise counsel of godly friends and family members.

Godly Decisions Involve the Heart

I was rather surprised when I learned from reading *Deadly Emotions* that the human heart has brainlike cells.[4] I had never heard that before. Dr. Colbert writes, "In recent years neurologists have discovered that the heart has its own independent brain-like system. At least 40,000 brain-type cell neurons exist in the human heart. That is the same amount found in various subordicals beneath the cerebral cortex centers of the brain. In other words, the heart is more than a mere biological pump. These abundant nerve cells give it thinking and feeling capabilities."[5]

During the 1970s, researchers John and Beatrice Lacey of the Fells Research Institute found that that the human heart can actually make decisions and talk to the brain. Fascinating! Research shows that the brain seems to obey the heart—contrary to popular thinking, which would have it the other way around. Dr. Colbert recommends that we talk out loud to our hearts. Though I don't fully understand this concept, I do pray out loud for every cell in my body to hear.

As I began to reflect on these studies regarding the heart, various proverbs came to mind:

A heart at peace gives life to the body, but envy rots the bones. (Proverbs 14:30)

A happy heart makes the face cheerful, but heartache crushes the spirit. (Proverbs 15:13)

The discerning heart seeks knowledge, but the mouth of a fool feeds on folly. (Proverbs 15:14)

A wise man's heart guides his mouth, and his lips promote instruction. (Proverbs 16:23)

A cheerful heart is good medicine, but a crushed spirit dries up the bones. (Proverbs 17:22)

Next, I thought about Ezekiel 11:19-20 (NKJV): "I will put a new spirit within them, and take the stony heart out of their flesh, and give them a heart of flesh, that they may walk in My statutes and keep My judgments and do them."

As I reflected on all the Lord had to say about this vital organ, I started listening to my heart, and I asked God to speak to me through my heart. My favorite verse that I have memorized is Colossians 3:15: "Let the peace of Christ rule in your hearts, since as members of one body you were called to peace." This verse makes it clear that the peace of Christ should rule our hearts.

Medical experts report that our hearts communicate messages

of well-being to our bodies through the release of helpful hormones and neurotransmitters. That might sound a bit technical to you and me, but as you've read some of the Scripture verses in this chapter, you've no doubt noticed how much God's Word attests to this medical fact. The most powerful channel of heart communication to the body is through the heart's electromagnetic field, which is about five thousand times greater in strength than the electromagnetic field produced by the brain.[6] When we realize that our hearts are electrically charged and more powerful than our brains, we are more apt to keep our hearts in tune with the Lord. The heart is very powerful. That is why the Bible says, "Above all else, guard your heart, for it is the wellspring of life."[7]

When we realize that our hearts are electrically charged and more powerful than our brains, we are more apt to keep our hearts in tune with the Lord.

Recently, my wife and I were trying to decide whether we should sell a small plot of land we owned on the lake in Branson. We had potential buyers, but we couldn't decide what to do. Neither of us had a peace about selling, but we didn't know why. We agreed that we would wait for God's peace to direct us, or we would make a decision not to sell. We received an offer from a qualified buyer, but still neither of us felt at peace. So, we didn't sell the land.

Two months later, one of our relatives called and said that he and his wife wanted to retire in Branson. He asked if we knew where they could find property near the lake. Norma and I just looked at each other with a smile and answered, "Yes, we do!" As I write these words, our relatives are walking the property to see about purchasing our land. Whether they purchase the land or not, we know we waited on the Lord for direction, and we have peace.

For many years of my ministry, I was too impatient to wait for God. I forgot what it was like to live with God's abiding peace; I only knew what it felt like to be driven and ruled by stress. From time to time I might have had some sense of peace, but I wasn't consciously surrendering my decisions to God. But now—wow!—what a joy it is to have God's unshakeable peace. I'm so aware of my frailty and helplessness that I can't imagine reverting back to making decisions on my own.

> For many years of my ministry, I was too impatient to wait for God. I forgot what it was like to live with God's abiding peace; I only knew what it felt like to be driven and ruled by stress.

For several years, I had days when I didn't know how I would be able to face my responsibilities, because there was so much pressure. Now, I see every moment that God gives me as a gift. I actually enjoy thinking about my upcoming speaking engagements, the books I'm writing, the meetings I'm going to have during the day, the times of interaction I'm going to have with my wife and family, and the playtime I'm going to have with my grandkids. I now have the energy to give of myself more freely. My commitment to include God in every important decision has changed my whole view of life.

Every morning, when I wake up, I ask God to speak to my heart and reveal his will for me that day in all I do and say. I ask him to empower me to listen to godly advisors before I make decisions. I want to be more like my wife, Norma: I want to be careful, thoughtful, and deliberate in making decisions. I used to be too impulsive. I would "shoot first and ask questions later." This tendency has caused me to wade in deep, troubling waters for most of my life. I've had to realize that my basic personality is not going to change. But that doesn't mean I'm a prisoner of my impulsive tendencies. It only means that I have to consciously surrender my impulsive tendencies—and a host of other tendencies—to the Lord each and every day.

Godly Decisions Take Time

On February 1, 2004, I learned another lesson about including God in all my decisions. I had been diligently trying to practice making prayerful decisions, but I was still learning to resist my impulsive inclinations. Once again, I learned the hard way about how *not* to make decisions.

I was scheduled to speak at a seminar in Springfield, Missouri, about thirty miles north of my home in Branson. I anticipated a great weekend because I knew the people who would be attending, and they were usually a great and responsive crowd. I arrived in town early and checked into my hotel about five hours before the seminar was to begin. I decided to drive around town and take in some of the sights. I had been thinking about buying a small motor home, and I said to myself, "Maybe I'll find one while I'm here."

I pulled into a big RV lot in town and soon located a used motor home. It was just the kind I wanted, and it seemed like a great price—the dealer was offering it for thirty percent off. It was an older model, a 1991, but it had a brand new engine and had been re-modeled inside. It looked great, had new carpet, and was very clean. I loved all the features, down to the hardwood paneling and oak cupboards.

"Wow, I don't want to pass up this deal," I said. So I called my wife and shared my enthusiasm with her. "Norm, I found this used motor home. You know how I've wanted one to go to seminars and other family trips. Boy, wouldn't it be fun in the summertime to take the kids over to the warm-water lake and camp there in our own RV? Maybe we could buy a little lot on the lake and enjoy the grandkids there. We could take trips every once in a while. What do you think?"

I was all worked up about the fun we were going to have with our family, and I got lost in my excitement. Norma was in a great mood, and I thought she was agreeing with what I was saying. But I realized later that I had totally misunderstood her.

> I was all worked up about the fun we were going to have with our family, and I got lost in my excitement.

After the seminar ended at noon on Saturday, I went back to the RV lot to put down a deposit. I called Norma and told her what I had done. I was pretty pumped up, and she also seemed excited about the idea. I looked at the RV once again and called my son Michael and some of my friends. They all seemed excited about it. Well, not everyone.

My good friend Jim Brawner is a great, Spirit-led man. I trusted his opinion. When I told him about the RV, he was a little hesitant and said, "Are you sure Norma likes this idea?" I went back to the RV lot and looked at the motor home again. I kept thinking, *This is such a great buy . . . and Norma seemed excited about it, too.* Finally, I decided to go ahead and start signing the papers. But now there was a slight check in my spirit.

I decided to call Norma again. She said, "No, I was just brainstorming with you. I wasn't serious about this. I really want to think this over and I want to discuss it with you. I want to use the new LUV Talk method of communication that we've learned over the last several years." (The LUV Talk method is explained in chapters 7 and 8 of my book *The DNA of Relationships.*)

I confessed, "Norm, the problem is I've already signed my name and put a deposit down. But I'll go back to see if I can get out of the contract."

I went back to the salesman, but by this time I was pretty embarrassed about the whole thing. I couldn't believe that I had misunderstood my wife and rushed into this. I had just started making strides to include God in my decision making, but I had clearly made a mistake here. I didn't have peace about it.

The general manager of the RV lot knew me, and when I walked back inside the office, he handed me his wife's copy of one of my books. "Would you autograph her book for me?"

Okay, now I was beyond embarrassed. I had given this man my word, and he knew about my ministry. I just kept thinking about how awkward it would be to back out of the deal. Finally, I convinced myself to take the RV home. I reasoned that it wouldn't cost me anything because I could probably sell it at a profit if Norma really didn't like it. But I convinced myself that she would like it, so I didn't have to worry about it.

The sales manager told me that if I didn't want the RV, now was the time to back out. I didn't back out, but I didn't have peace about it, either. I was stuck because of my own embarrassment. All the way home I was thinking, *What an idiot I am. How dense can I possibly be to rush into something like this?* Talk about buyer's remorse! And I wasn't even home yet. I should have just swallowed my pride and said to the sales manager, "I'll go home and talk to my wife about it again, and I'll get back to you and let you know what we decide." I could have been out of a mess that was only going to get worse.

While driving home in the RV, I kept hearing a funny sound

> I was beyond embarrassed. I had given this man my word, and he knew about my ministry. I just kept thinking about how awkward it would be to back out of the deal.

that I had not noticed on the test drive. I even pulled over at one point and looked under the hood to see if I noticed anything. The hood barely held on to the socket, and I made a mental note to get that fixed.

I didn't back out, but I didn't have peace about it, either. I was stuck because of my own embarrassment.

Once I got home, the excitement took over again, and I could not wait to show Norma. I pulled up in our backyard and honked the horn. She came out and stepped into the RV through the side door. "What do you think, Norm?" I said. She was silent. I showed her the bedroom and the shower. It had a small refrigerator and a microwave. Her first words were, "I am not staying overnight in this thing." I had to admit that it had a unique smell, but I thought it could be remedied with some aerosol spray.

My kids were excited about having access to a motor home. Roger and Kari were the first to call to borrow it. They got their stuff packed and planned to take it into nearby Arkansas to camp someplace by a stream and a mountain. Their kids had all their toys and video games, and the food was loaded for a four-day trip. When they left, I had a great feeling of confidence that finally someone would appreciate the purchase I had made.

Less than ten minutes later, I got a phone call from Kari. "Dad, it's horrible!" she said.

"What, Kari? What is horrible?" I asked.

"The motor home has broken down, and we are in the middle of an intersection. The traffic light has changed, but we can't move, and the hood has smoke billowing out from under it."

I rushed across town to where they were, and sure enough, the spark plug cords had gotten too hot and had melted onto the engine. I called to have the RV towed to the repair shop and helped Kari and

Roger unpack the motor home into my pickup for the ride back home. Their faces showed their disappointment about not being able to go on their trip. I took them all to a movie and dinner that night to try to get them to stop thinking about it, but after that experience, no one dared to borrow the motor home. It became, like many RVs, a fixture in the backyard.

After I got everything fixed, I did manage to talk one of my staff members into borrowing the RV. He and his family got past the main stoplight in town, but as they got out on the highway, he noticed that the motor home kept pulling to the right. When it started to rain, the pulling became

> After that experience, no one dared to borrow the motor home. It became, like many RVs, a fixture in the backyard.

dangerous because it was hard to keep the vehicle straight on the road. After a few miles of that, they pulled to the side of the road and canceled their trip.

When Norma heard the news, she told me that the motor home had to be sold. After a few weeks, I found a buyer and could not wait to deposit the check.

When I got home, Norma asked me, "How did it go?"

I told her that the buyer had liked it and bought it.

"How much did we make?" she asked.

"Well . . . let's just say I could start a new business where I buy things high and sell them low," I said. "We lost almost $10,000."

Norma was silent.

Once again I went back to listening to what God had been speaking to my heart: Seek godly counsel in decision making. Take time for decisions to "settle." Pay attention to "checks" in your spirit. Don't move forward without the peace of God. I think back to the day I bought the motor home—I was so excited at the prospect of owning the RV that I lost perspective. Without really praying about it, I purchased it. Without further counsel from godly friends, I made a rash decision. I went against what I knew God was teaching me.

Seek godly counsel in decision making. Take time for decisions to "settle." Pay attention to "checks" in your spirit. Don't move forward without the peace of God.

Because of the motor home fiasco, Norma and I decided that we would consult with each other and come to explicit agreement before making purchases over a certain dollar amount. There would be no more "I think Norma will like this after she's gotten used to the idea." We've also agreed that we will consult with some of our good friends whom we trust to be good stewards before we make a final decision on a major purchase. This system has been a good checks-and-balances approach for us and has saved me from buying anything under pressure. Through this difficult experience, I have become better at slowing down and asking myself the following questions:

- Is my heart being ruled by the peace of God?
- Am I really following God's will?
- Have I asked godly friends for counsel?
- Does Norma agree with the decision?

With my personality, I still come up with a lot of "great ideas" that I want to follow up on immediately. But I'm learning—and I think I'm getting better at this—to listen to Norma and to other wise counselors, which has led to a series of sound decisions. I want to listen to my wife and live out our service to the Lord in agreement with each other. I want to wait upon the Lord every day so that my strength is renewed and I benefit from his unsurpassed wisdom. "I can do all things through Christ who strengthens me."[8] As I "trust in the LORD with all [my] heart and lean not on [my] own understanding," he will guide me.[9]

Godly Decisions Require Prayerful Empathy

Prayer is our lifeline connection to God. Without daily communication, we will be less inclined to realize our need for him. I don't know what your schedule is like, but I know that each one of my days has a list of demands that can steal my heart away from first seeking God if I'm not careful. The temptation is to think we can do everything at once. Perhaps multitasking is your specialty. But I'd like to challenge you to find a quiet place and prayerfully ask God to show you how your decisions are affecting other people. When we consider the burdens that weigh on other people, our prayers become less selfish—and in turn, our decisions become less selfish as well.

> I began to reflect on the struggles of being in ministry together and the various experiences we had been through as a family. I decided to listen to my heart and to God.

Here is a fresh example that happened recently. When I went to bed at ten o'clock one night, my wife was already asleep. I took advantage of this quiet time and started listening to my heart. I needed to make a decision with my son Greg about our partnership in ministry. I knew that the impact of this decision was going to affect many of my loved ones.

Greg had said to me a few days before that he didn't feel that I really understood some of the struggles he had been through in the previous year regarding his work and how my interaction with what he does affected him. He said he was dealing with deep emotional pain. I began to reflect on the struggles of being in ministry together and the various experiences we had been through as a family. I decided to listen to my heart and to God to help me understand Greg's emotional pain so that I could have more compassion for him. I asked God to give me more compassion and understanding for Greg and his wife, Erin, and their children.

I reviewed in my heart and mind what Greg had gone through over the course of the year. I put myself in his shoes and mentally walked through the difficult months of struggle that I knew about. When I started to realize the weight of his burdens, I was moved with emotion and compassion. I knew he had felt like a failure a couple of times, and as his father I knew that was one of his core fears, as it is for many men. I thought about how Greg must have felt among his peers and close friends. I played out in my mind how he would have responded to Erin and his children, how he would have responded to his staff. I started feeling deep emotions and remembered people in my own past who had hurt me deeply.

Next, I prayerfully reflected on my relationship with my son-in-law, Roger, and my daughter, Kari. I remembered some of their pain, and I recalled some of their trials. I thought about the struggles that parenting can bring to a young couple's life, and how well Roger and Kari loved their children. My eyes teared up as I prayed for them, asking God to help them in all their decisions as parents.

Then I thought about Norma's struggles, not the least of which was having to live with me all these years. I felt some of her pain from the past year in particular. I was more acquainted with her painful issues than I was with my kids', but I realized that I didn't fully understand how difficult the year had been for her. I thought about many decisions I had made that profoundly affected her life. For example, when I had decided to retire and give my ministry over to my children, I hadn't even consulted her, even though she was the vice president. I recalled one terribly devastating staff meeting where we dealt with some of the structural changes. It was a severe blow to her, and I needed to be confronted with the pain she endured as a result of my hasty decisions. Some of her pain was due to my selfish way of making decisions and my failure to heed her warnings.

Finally, I thought about my son Michael and his wife, Amy. I stayed awake until two o'clock that morning thinking about my family. I knew my falling away from God throughout the 1990s had deeply affected our family relationships. I listened carefully to God's Spirit leading my heart, and I felt that he increased the level of compassion I had for my family and my friends.

> I thought about many decisions I had made that profoundly affected Norma's life.

By the time I met with Greg the next morning, I felt like I had been living his life over the past two years, that I did feel his pain, and that I did see how he had been affected. As our eyes met, before either one of us had said a word, he could tell I understood. His first words were, "Dad, I just needed you to understand me, and I see that you do."

We talked about the decision at hand for a while, and then, as we always do, we sent e-mails back and

> Doing business with family members is never easy, and extra prayer is often required.

forth with our thoughts of how to proceed. Within a few days, we had an agreement that we both had peace about.

Doing business with family members is never easy, and extra

prayer is often required. If you find yourself needing to make an important decision that involves your family or close friends, adopting a posture of prayerful empathy may help you act with a greater measure of wisdom. God has graciously given me insight that I would not have gained without the power of prayer.

Godly Decisions Require Focused Listening

Though I am a communicator by trade, I'm still learning how to do it better. I have come to a place in my life where I realize that the most important element of communication is *listening*. Probably 90 percent of our communication with other people rises and falls on our ability to hear them and understand their feelings and needs. When we take time to understand and sincerely value what the other person is saying, it saves much time later on. James tells us, "My dear brothers, take note of this: Everyone should be quick to listen, slow to speak and slow to become angry."[10] We must *listen* and *understand* before we even think about *doing*.

> I try not to take anything personally. I try to hear, understand, and value what the person is saying before I ever try to respond.

How much time and money would I have saved if I had really understood Norma's feelings about the motor home? It is easy not to listen in a conversation, to only care about being understood by the other person.

Today, when I enter a conversation, I try not to come with any prejudgment. I try not to listen with a critical ear. I try not to take anything personally. I try to hear, understand, and value what the person is saying before I ever try to respond.

One day, I had a conversation with Dr. Bob Paul, copresident and CEO of the National Institute of Marriage, which grew out of

Bob's involvement in the Smalley Marriage Institute. He was the key designer of several of the relationship strategies I discuss in my book *The DNA of Relationships*. As we began to partner on another project, I asked Bob how he could feel like a total winner in every aspect of our collaboration. Then I asked, "What are three of your top concerns, which if I understood them, would make you feel like we could partner together?"

Whenever I ask people to tell me their top three concerns, the whole conversation changes and they are usually delighted to share with me. When Bob saw that I truly wanted to understand him, I could see his body relax and we went on to an agreeable contract.

As I went back over each one of his three concerns, I began to ask more specific questions. "What do you mean by this first one?" I began to draw out of him, in further detail, what he was saying. I wanted him to know that I really understood what he needed. I wanted to wait until I had heard as much as possible before I asked him the golden question: "Do you feel as if I understand enough about your concerns to move forward in negotiating a contract?"

> When we really communicate with people through careful listening, they automatically feel valued.

When we really communicate with people through careful listening, they automatically feel valued. Perhaps you are someone who easily misinterprets what other people say. This has happened to me many times, so I have learned to pause. Then I repeat back to them what I think they are saying, using different words or a series of different words and phrases. This gives me time and opportunity to fully comprehend what they have said.

Sometimes I inject word pictures. When I know a friend is

facing a problem, I might ask, "How does this struggle make you feel? Paint a word picture for me." He or she might say, "It feels like I've been shot with a high-powered rifle and I'm limping home. I don't know why I was shot, and I'm bleeding pretty badly. I think I'm going to make it home in time to live, but I'm wounded and in pain."

Whether I agree or disagree with the other person's point of view, I remind myself that he or she is very valuable to God, and therefore worthy of my respect and consideration. In any communication, I want all parties to feel as if they are winning. I want to be a teammate, not a tyrant. I don't want to feel like I'm losing in a discussion, and neither should anyone else. Above all, I want to come to a point where we all experience God's peace.

To further illustrate this point, I'll give you another example from the motor home incident. (Can you tell I learned a lot from that experience?) When Norma and I began discussing what we should do with the RV, I wanted to keep it, and she didn't. We started reflecting on her concerns. She said, "I feel we have too many things to maintain today, and we don't have enough time. Our ministry is growing rapidly. We are so busy. The motor home is just one more thing to maintain. We have to license it, insure it, winterize it, and on and on. There are so many things that I have to do because I am the accountant and the detail manager. If I can't do all of them, you have to step in and do them, which takes you away from the ministry; that grieves me."

> In any communication, I want all parties to feel as if they are winning. I want to be a teammate, not a tyrant.

I understood what she was saying, and she was right. We were too busy. At that point, we owned too many gadgets and couldn't even have found the time to enjoy the RV. Our toys owned us instead of our owning them.

Then Norma listened to me as I explained my reasons for wanting to keep the RV. I mentioned how much easier it would be to travel to seminars that were close by. Instead of driving all the way to the airport and flying to these cities, I could just drive to the cities. It would make my travel quicker. Plus, I would have a place to sleep along the way, if necessary.

I gave her all my reasons, and I felt that she understood. I felt that she valued me and that I was valuing her.

Then I said, "So, what's the solution?"

Norma said, "While you were sharing your point of view, I had an idea. What if every time you need to use a motor home for travel to a seminar that's less than ten hours away by car, why not just rent one? There's a rental company just a few miles from here. Let's try that for six months or so. If we come to realize that we really need to own an RV, we can buy a newer one. And we'll be able to deduct taxes for the whole thing because we'll be using it for our ministry."

I felt like a winner, and she did too. I felt that she understood me and that she was cooperating with me by suggesting the rental. We soon found that there were many other benefits to this compromise. By renting an RV, I don't have any mainte-nance costs or responsibilities. If the motor home I'm driving breaks down, the company comes and fixes it. It's pretty much a win-win solution for all of us. This conversation gave Norma and me a peaceful resolution to our di-lemma and allowed us to do some "treasure hunting" as well. What started as a trial turned into a good solution that I'm still benefiting from today.

> I felt like a winner, and she did too. I felt that she understood me and that she was cooperating with me.

I can now say that I really try to listen carefully to Norma. I listen to her more than ever before. I try to listen carefully to my friends, to my heart, and to Scripture. When I do this, I'm much more apt to hear and heed the voice of God.

Godly Decisions Consider the Past

Reminiscing seems to help me understand someone if we have a history together and we are trying to make a serious decision. My wife and I have had many great experiences together, including times with our family. For example, I remember the songs I used to play on the cassette deck in my mini motor home when my kids were small. As we would drive across the country, Kari and I would sing a John Denver song or an Andy Williams tune at the top of our lungs while the boys played Nerf football in the back. These were some of the happiest times of my life, and I treasure the memories.

When I am in the middle of deciding something important with any of my children, I often bring up the past to help us decide.

Now when I am in the middle of deciding something important with any of my children, I often bring up the past to help us decide. Kari e-mailed me recently for advice about her son. Sometimes he forgets to bring home his schoolwork. That really frustrates my daughter. As you might imagine, I reminded her of what she was like when she was in school. We talked about what is really valuable in life and she agreed that schoolwork is very important, but not as important as her son's character and love for God. He is so unique and mature for his age, and we talk about the burden that goes along with such maturity. I reminded her of who her son is, and what he has already done of great importance in his young life.

Kari remembered her own school days, which I can proudly

attest made her the envy of any father, and she decided to get off her son's case and start enjoying what he has become instead of riding him so often about his schoolwork.

I also remember having some great conversations with my children while we were driving down the road. We would be on some desolate highway in Oklahoma or Texas and just start talking with each other about anything. The miles flew by. Even today, I put old songs on my CD player, close my eyes (not when I'm driving), and remember my family growing up. We had so much fun and did so many things together. It cheers me up and reminds me of what is really important in life.

I like to reminisce about life in general. I go back and remind myself of the miracles that God has done in my life. Remembering is an important part of our Christian experience. Our history is sacred with God. Our past often can help us make better decisions in the future. Through all the tough, tough times in ministry, I do not have to look hard to find God's grace surrounding me. So many people have mentored and taught me during my lifetime. God has given me countless opportunities to share his principles in places all over the world. He has opened so many doors for me through books and videos, and he has answered so many prayers from couples to save their marriages. The blessings are endless. Miracles and answers to prayers in the past give me confidence in him today and for the future. He has always been faithful. What a legacy we have as a family. I am humbled to know that I can never take credit for it, because God did it all.

Reminiscing often helped the people of God. Take a glance

> We had so much fun and did so many things together. It cheers me up when I remember what is really important in life.

through the Bible and see all the references to God's relationship with his people. Their toilsome, wild, radical, troubled past was all part of their journey together. God wanted his people to remember all they had endured so that they would remember him. Through the desert wanderings, through the rebuilding of Jerusalem's wall, through good and evil kings, through the trials and tribulations of the early church—our history as God's people matters today. Many times, God's people would build an altar just to remember God's goodness and how he had delivered them from their enemies. Throughout the Psalms, David remembers the goodness of God. Jesus asks us to remember him and his sacrifice. The command to "remember" is a command of great significance. When we reflect on our experiences with God, we are more apt to learn from the past and make better choices in the future.

> When we reflect on our experiences with God, we are more apt to learn from the past and make better choices in the future.

The Israelites often found themselves in a familiar cycle with God. They would stray, repent, and be restored. Though they continued to make the same mistakes, God repeatedly showed them mercy. His covenant with them could not be broken, even when they were unfaithful. Such a history is important to us today. We can learn a lot from the poor choices made by God's people. We can gain wisdom by studying the history of God's people and their efforts to live for him.

The practice of remembering is a very important part of my life. I still have decisions to face that I'm unsure about from time to time, but God always gives me his counsel and the counsel of those I trust. He wants us to involve him in the daily decisions of our lives. When we involve God in our decisions, we involve him in our lives, and that is what he wants. Once you do this, you will be amazed at how your relationship with him flourishes.

YOUR RELATIONSHIP WITH GOD

1. What hinders you from taking time to seek out godly counsel in your life?

2. Think about a time in your life when you made a bad decision. What were the consequences? Who was affected?

3. Do you think God wants to be included in every decision of your life? What kind of decisions in life do you think require godly counsel?

KEY PASSAGE: Read James 3:13-17

James talks about two kinds of wisdom. Apply this passage to a specific decision you are facing. Ask God to give you wisdom from heaven.

MAKING IT PERSONAL

Make a list of people you respect who would take time to help you make a decision that you feel requires the counsel of others. Do what you can to strengthen your relationships with godly people and surround yourself with wise friends.

8

REVIEWING YOUR
RELATIONSHIP WITH GOD

I'll never forget asking a very popular Christian leader how he maintained his walk with Christ each day. He seemed like a serious person most of the time, but he floored me when he looked deep into my eyes and said, "Surely you know the answer. It's review, review, review, stupid." Stunned, I shot back with another question, "Was the *stupid* intended for me, or was it a testimony from you?" We both had a good laugh.

I don't know anyone who can maintain a good relationship with anyone without continual communication and contact. I can't get out of bed in the morning without reviewing what is going on between God and me. I do the same thing at night, reviewing my day with him. I also occasionally reflect on my words and actions throughout the course of the day, asking God to mold me into his likeness.

When I am discouraged, I take time to remember how God

was faithful the day before, and I review the promises he has made in his Word. I'm often quite humbled by how quickly and easily I forget everything that God has done for me. Some days, I need constant reminders.

When I am discouraged, I take time to remember how God was faithful the day before, and I review the promises he has made in his Word.

A while ago, I remember having a low-level ache in my heart. I knew that something was unsettled in me, but I couldn't put my finger on it. One night, I cried out to God to show me what was causing this anxiety. I finally fell asleep after a while, with no answers. The next morning, I awoke with the same uneasy feeling. I reviewed my favorite verses, but the feeling didn't change. On my way to an appointment that morning, I called my wife and told her what I was feeling. She paused and responded with this question: "How many unfinished things do you have on your plate today?" I thought about it for a moment and I told her that I hadn't counted lately.

"Why don't you go home after your meeting and write everything down on one sheet of paper?" Norma suggested.

When I did that, I filled an entire sheet of paper, spilling my list outside the margins. No wonder my heart was sick. My list of things to do looked totally overwhelming. The first thing I did was call my two personal assistants and begged for their help. They calmed me down by explaining what they were already doing about most of my list. As I was thanking God for my two able assistants, I realized that he was demonstrating his faithfulness to me, and I didn't have to be all tied up in a knot about everything. In a fresh, new way, I was able to let go of my long list and trust God to guide my steps. I had to take time to remember that God was faithful and that he was greater than

REVIEWING YOUR RELATIONSHIP WITH GOD

everything that was on my plate. I had to remember that all the things he wanted me to do I could do with his help and strength.

How I Start My Day

Will you allow me to ask you a very serious question? How much time do you spend each day reflecting with God, reviewing his Word, studying and memorizing his revealed truth?

Estimate your average allotted time: _____.

Are you satisfied with the amount you wrote down? If not, think about a reasonable amount of time you could work toward spending with God: _____.

For me, I need to take at least an hour each morning in order to feel equipped to start my day. It is so easy to think we don't have time for God. But it is really quite arrogant to think we don't have time for our Creator and Lord, the God of the universe. Seriously, what could be more important in your life than spending time with God?

Don't misunderstand. I haven't forgotten my own story of wandering away from God, so I'm not wagging my finger at you. But if you've allowed your job, your spouse, your children, your hobbies, or just plain busyness to crowd time for God out of your life, let me gently encourage you to rethink your priorities. Start today, and give God as much time as he needs to give you the spiritual food that you need.

Start today, and give God as much time as he needs to give you the spiritual food that you need.

Here's what I recommend to keep your relationship with God healthy: Engage him in conversation as soon as you wake up, and right before you go to bed at night.

I'm not suggesting that you have to spend an hour with God

every morning before you even get out of bed. But I am saying that my day gets off on the right foot when I take time to review my relationship with God before I get caught up in my schedule for the day. I spend enough time to at least go through my favorite verses and pray them back to God. It might be ten minutes one morning and an hour the next. I try to take time to listen and pray until I feel that God has given me the spiritual food I need for the day. Without review, I tend to slip back into my old ruts and patterns of living. If I'm not careful, it can take just one day for me to forget God's faithfulness.

I encourage you to spend as much time as it takes for you to be alone with God and review your walk with him. Once you get in the habit of walking through these steps, you will see how easily the Spirit maximizes the time you devote to God. If you're not used to doing this, start off with five minutes. You'll be amazed how quickly the time goes. As you get into the habit of starting your day with God, you will probably want to set your alarm a little earlier each day. I set my heart at peace each morning by reviewing five basic checkpoints:

1. I review who God is.
2. I pray, and I review how God has answered my prayers.
3. I review the facts that God lives in my heart and that he has called me to serve him.
4. I review what God is saying to me.
5. I review how I have grown.

Here are a few suggestions for how you can incorporate this five-point review into your morning routine.

REVIEW WHO GOD IS. Reviewing who God is gets your focus immediately on him. Ask yourself what attributes of God are especially meaningful to you right now in your life. Use the names of God to remind yourself of his character and nature: God is good. God is your shield. God is your fortress. God is your rear guard. God is your life. God is your strength. (See the appendix for a list of more than one hundred names for God that can encourage and inspire you.) Take time to meditate on what Scripture says about God. (For starters, read Psalm 59:9; Nahum 1:7; John 3:16; 2 Corinthians 12:9; Ephesians 3:18; and 1 John 4:9-10.)

When I am reminded of who God is, I see life from a much more realistic perspective. Left to my own devices, I can easily think something is more important than it really is. But when I take time to reflect on God's character and nature, my attitude and my priorities fall into line.

> I am bending my knee
> In the eye of the Father who created me,
> In the eye of the Son who purchased me,
> In the eye of the Spirit who cleansed me,
> In friendship and affection.
> —A Celtic tune

> Praise the Lord! Praise the Lord, O my soul! I will
> praise the Lord as long as I live; I will sing praises to
> my God all my life long. Do not put your trust in
> princes, in mortals, in whom there is no help. When
> their breath departs, they return to the earth; on that
> very day their plans perish. Happy are those whose help
> is the God of Jacob, whose hope is in the Lord their
> God, who made heaven and earth, the sea, and all that is
> in them; who keeps faith forever; who executes justice
> for the oppressed; who gives food to the hungry. The

Lord sets the prisoners free; the Lord opens the eyes of
the blind. The Lord lifts up those who are bowed down;
the Lord loves the righteous. The Lord watches over the
strangers; he upholds the orphan and the widow, but the
way of the wicked he brings to ruin. The Lord will reign
forever, your God, O Zion, for all generations. Praise the
Lord! (Psalm 146:1-10, NRSV)

PRAY, AND REVIEW HOW GOD HAS ANSWERED YOUR
PRAYERS. At times, we all feel as if our prayers are just bouncing
off the walls, never quite making it past the ceiling. But we know
that God hears every prayer. He is always faithful to listen to us,
even when we feel alone in prayer. At such times, I remind myself
how God has proved to me over and over again that he honors persistence and he really does answer prayer.

Remember the parable that Jesus tells in Luke 18 about the
persistent widow? She kept coming to the unrighteous judge, seeking his mercy for her plight. For a while, the judge was unwilling to
help her, but finally he gave the legal protection she wanted. Who
knows how long she pleaded with him before the judge recognized
her determined spirit? Jesus then says the life-changing words for
me, "And will not God bring about justice for his chosen ones, who
cry out to him day and night?" (v. 7).

I remember how God gave my family a new car years ago,
when Kari was a teenager, after she and I had prayed for almost a
year. It was at a time when our finances were very tight and our car
was definitely on its last legs. Kari and I prayed together every
night for God's help. One day, a family friend happened to drive our
car. As he sank into the broken driver's seat, he said, "This is pa-
thetic; no friend of mine should be driving something like this. Tomorrow, we're going to whatever car lot you want and I'm buying

you a new car." God's provision came right out of the blue (*heaven's blue*). Kari and I knew that God had heard each and every prayer we had prayed. I have so many stories like this one that I can review, and by the end of just one of these, I am so much more confident that my current prayers will be answered—in God's way and in his timing. As I pray, I remember Christ's words from the garden of Gethsemane: "Not my will, but yours be done."[1] I don't want anything that is not consistent with God's Word or his will.

Prayer requires focus and commitment. Focus requires centering in on God. If we're not careful, the busyness of our lives can become a never-ending excuse not to pray. Emilie Griffin says, "There is a moment between intending to pray and actually praying that is as dark and silent as any moment in our lives. It is the split second between thinking about prayer and really praying. For some of us, this split second may last for decades. It seems, then, that the generational obstacle to prayer is the simple matter of beginning, the simple exertion of the will, the starting, the acting, the doing."[2]

> Prayer requires focus and commitment. Focus requires centering in on God. If we're not careful, the busyness of our lives can become a never-ending excuse not to pray.

Many of us want to pray more often, but we rarely slow down long enough to come into God's presence. This was certainly true of me for many years. God calls us to cease from our activities long enough to spend time with him. James writes, "Come near to God and he will come near to you. Wash your hands, you sinners, and purify your hearts, you double-minded."[3] As we purify ourselves and come near to God in prayer, and he comes near to us, he will transform our lives by renewing our minds. "Then you will be able to test and approve what God's will is—his good, pleasing and perfect will."[4] Eighteenth-century author William Law wrote of the inner transformation that occurs when we devote ourselves to our relationship with God: "This Pearl of Eternity is the Church, or Temple of God within Thee, the consecrated Place of Divine Worship, where alone thou canst worship God in Spirit, and in Truth. . . . When once thou art well grounded in this inward Worship, thou wilt have learnt to live unto God above Time, and Place. For every Day will be Sunday to thee, and wherever thou goest, thou wilt have a Priest, a Church, and an Altar along with Thee."[5] Law's wording is old-fashioned (this quote is from a book first published in 1749), but his message is timeless and very powerful. As Christians, when we become "well grounded in this inward Worship," we create within ourselves the ability to come into the presence of God, regardless of time or place. That's the power of regular, persistent prayer.

REVIEW THE FACTS THAT GOD LIVES IN YOUR HEART AND THAT HE HAS CALLED YOU TO SERVE HIM. Many Scriptures attest to the fact that God resides within us, has brought us into his family, and has a purpose for our lives. (For starters, read Psalm 17:7-8; Matthew 28:19-20; John 1:12; 14:27; 15:15-16; Ephesians 2:8-9; 3:16-19; 1 John 5:11.) He is there to provide peace and power if we have made Jesus Lord of our lives. Meditate on verses that help you to take hold of that truth. I never get out of bed without saying these words: "Thank you, Lord, for sending your Spirit to live within my heart. Thank you for your power and love that are in me."

"Therefore, since we are justified by faith, we have peace with God through our Lord Jesus Christ, through whom we have obtained access to this grace in which we stand; and we boast in our hope of sharing the glory of God."[6] God has called us to himself. We have been bought with a price. Because of Jesus, the Holy Spirit lives within us so we have great reason to rejoice.

Watchman Nee, a leader in the indigenous church movement in China until his death in 1973, writes in his book *The Normal Christian Life*: "Do you realize what happened at your conversion? God came into your heart and made it his temple. In Solomon's days God dwelt in a temple made of stone: today he dwells in a temple composed of living believers. When we really see that God has made our hearts His dwelling-place, what a deep reverence will come over our lives!"[7]

"Do you realize what happened at your conversion? God came into your heart and made it his temple."

REVIEW WHAT GOD IS SAYING TO YOU. I cannot overemphasize the importance of reading God's Word every day, with the sole purpose of getting to know him better. I believe it is essential to our relationship with God. Here are a few suggestions for how to organize your time:

- Take time to read a verse or passage several times and ask God to help you listen. Ask the core questions: what? when? where? how? who? and why?
- Study particular words in more detail. Look up other passages with those words. Memorize one or two verses that you can repeat the next morning.
- Listen. Quiet your heart to allow the Holy Spirit to speak to you through God's Word. Consider what the Holy Spirit brings to your attention and how it fits with the rest of the Bible and life in general.
- Move from meditation to application—connect your

thoughts to action. Consider how the truth and power of God's Word should affect your behavior today.

In today's hurry-up culture, it's easy to get so busy that we spend less and less time in the Bible. But we really have more opportunities to hear or read God's Word than ever before. We can hear messages on the radio, through the Internet, through audio copies, through conferences, through Bible studies, and especially through our churches. There have been periods in my life when I thought I had heard all the messages one could hear in a lifetime. My heart became hard to learning fresh new insights and letting God speak to me through his Word. That was foolish. None of us should ever think we are so spiritually self-sufficient that we don't need to hear or read God's Word daily. Just as we need physical food each day, we also need spiritual food each day.

> Blessed is the one who reads the words of this prophecy, and blessed are those who hear it and take to heart what is written in it, because the time is near. (Revelation 1:3)

> Your word is a lamp to my feet and a light to my path. (Psalm 119:105, NKJV)

> All scripture is inspired by God and is useful for teaching, for reproof, for correction, and for training in righteousness, so that everyone who belongs to God may be proficient, equipped for every good work. (2 Timothy 3:16-17, NRSV)

REVIEW HOW YOU HAVE GROWN. As you put these steps into action, you may find yourself getting discouraged from time to time.

Maybe you push the snooze button one too many times and miss starting your day with God. Don't get discouraged. No matter what happens, keep making time for God, and make time to review how you have grown in your relationship with him.

Each morning, I spend five minutes or so reviewing what happened in the past twenty-four hours that affected me. I reflect on how I wish I had responded in various situations, and I ask God to give me the strength to act differently in the future. It is important to take time to confess your sins to God and experience his forgiveness. You've heard it said that every day is the first day of the rest of your life. Make each day count. God's grace is sufficient.

> Each morning, I spend five minutes or so reviewing what happened in the past twenty-four hours that affected me.

Here are some questions to ask yourself:

- What did God teach me yesterday about my life?
- What is God refining, sharpening, confronting in me?
- How did God use me yesterday for his service?
- How did I use my spiritual gifts to love others?

Godly growth and character are by-products of our daily walk with God. Calvin Miller said, "You can buy personality cheap, but character is not for sale. Character grows by God's power in us each day through everything we experience. Character comes gradually in the process of allowing God to make us servants."[8]

The apostle Paul reveals the secret to godly character: "I have been crucified with Christ; it is no longer I who live, but Christ lives in me; and the life which I now live in the flesh I live by faith in the Son of God, who loved me and gave Himself for me."[9]

The apostle Peter puts it this way: "In this you greatly rejoice, though now for a little while you may have had to suffer grief in all kinds of trials. These have come so that your faith—of greater worth than gold, which perishes even though refined by fire—may be proved genuine and may result in praise, glory and honor when Jesus Christ is revealed."[10]

Other verses you may want to review (and memorize) include Psalm 55:16-17; Matthew 11:28; Romans 5:3-5; 1 Corinthians 16:13; Philippians 3:20-21; and Hebrews 12:7-11.

Our relationship with God is always a work in progress. It is never finished. It changes daily. Growth happens even when we can't detect it. There is no such thing as standing still in our journey with God. We are either growing closer to him, or we are regressing and moving away from him. Paul writes, "Train yourself to be godly. For physical training is of some value, but godliness has value for all things, holding promise for both the present life and the life to come."[11]

Training involves practice and persistence. Paul also writes, "Not that I have already obtained all this, or have already been made perfect, but I press on to take hold of that for which Christ Jesus took hold of me."[12] We must press on throughout each day, listening and responding to God.

A Final Word

Looking back on my life from my present vantage point, there is no place I would rather be than where I am right now. We all have our different life experiences, but what we have in common is an inherent hunger for a closer walk with God. No matter how many other things we think will satisfy us, nothing is more fulfilling than our relationship with God. You've read about some of the vain pursuits that led to my spiritual decline. You've read about the pride and arrogance that kept me from growing in my relationship with God for several years. I was distracted by success, which crowded out my hunger for God. Ironically, God's blessing and favor on my life turned out to be the very thing I allowed to come between us. Perhaps there is something that is coming between you and God that you need to surrender to him. My prayer is that God will speak to you through what happened to me.

Do not let success, wealth, busyness, distractions, or any of your ambitions crowd out your hunger for God. Idols come in all forms, shapes, and sizes. Sometimes they sneak into our lives, and we don't even notice they are competing for first place in our hearts. But don't give in. You can resist temptation to dethrone God; you can have the relationship with God you've always dreamed of.

> Do not let success, wealth, busyness, distractions, or any of your ambitions crowd out your hunger for God.

Tragically, I was wooed by the sirens of success and self-sufficiency. I really thought I could handle it— I even felt entitled to it. I should have known better. Don't listen to what the world tells you will satisfy you. Money, fame, power are all fleeting. The truth is that our lives are also fleeting; we are here today and gone tomorrow. But that isn't the whole story. We were created to have a close walk with God, both now and throughout eternity. Start today to live in a way that matters to God.

I urge you to pursue the abundant life that God promises

through a dynamic, growing relationship with Jesus Christ. Pray for God to release you from worldly expectations. Let Christ set you free from the bondage of selfish materialism and the temptations of our culture and society. Turn aside from anything that is keeping you from pursuing a closer relationship with God.

Align your heart with God's words. Ask God to expose the lies you are believing about your life, yourself, and others. Stop blaming other people for the failures in your life; instead, adopt a heart of gratitude and humility toward God. Thank him for the blessings he has poured out on your life—including the gift of life itself.

> Stop blaming other people for the failures in your life; instead, adopt a heart of gratitude and humility toward God.

And remember, God is in control no matter what happens. He will open and close doors and see you through the trials that life brings, working everything out for your good. Trust his plan for your life and commit yourself to him.

Communication with God is the key to having the relationship with him you've always wanted. Make sure you are talking to him every day; reading his Word; and reviewing his character, attributes, and faithfulness. Praise God all the time, thanking him for being a loving God who desires a close relationship with his children.

Above all, remember that God knows you and loves you right where you are. He doesn't want you to wait a second longer to make things right with him. He knows exactly what you need and when you need it. He is our Great Shepherd, guiding his sheep into green pastures. He can lead us out of the tall grass, where we can't see, away from the cliff. Trust him to show you the way. Also, it's important to realize that we were never meant to live out the Christian life alone. Surround yourself with godly counsel and wisdom. Listen to your pastor, your teachers, and others who walk closely with the Lord.

I know it would be easy for you to set this book aside and never take action on what I've suggested. But I don't want you to do that. My hope is that you will see this moment as a new beginning and not an ending. Don't miss the opportunity that you have right now to draw closer in your relationship with God. Let me challenge you to start your day—every day—with God.

Above all, remember that God knows you and loves you right where you are.

To help you get started, I've included ten brief meditations on Colossians 3:1-17, the verses God used to rekindle my relationship with him (see page 141). I have a long way to go, but I encourage you to join me on the journey to a closer relationship with God. I'm preparing to meet him face-to-face one day, but I'm not waiting for heaven to enjoy a relationship with him. I'm drawing closer to him every day right now.

Let me pray for your relationship with God:

Lord, I pray that you would help my brothers and sisters to recognize that their lives are hidden with Christ in you, and that you have raised them up, away from the world's ways and desires. Help all of us to clothe ourselves with compassion, kindness, humility, gentleness, and patience through the power of your Spirit at work in us. May we live lives of gratitude, with you at the center.

In Jesus' name,

Amen

YOUR RELATIONSHIP WITH GOD

1. Think about a relationship in your life that has been particularly difficult. How do you wish you could communicate with this person? What do you think God is trying to teach you through this relationship?

2. Trace the course of your day yesterday. List the ways in which you witnessed God at work in your life.

3. What verses have been particularly meaningful to you when you've needed a reminder that God is faithful?

KEY VERSES: Deuteronomy 6:4-9
Ask God to help you remember him in all situations.

MAKING IT PERSONAL
Journal your memories of some of the most intimate moments you have known with God. Recall how you felt during those times in your life. Write down how remembering your past with God strengthens your future with him.

MEDITATIONS ON
COLOSSIANS 3

Before my revival, I had become too distracted to experience the full impact of God's Word in my life. I had set up too many idols around my heart—my expectations, my goals, my book sales, the success of my ministry, my comfortable lifestyle, my fancy vacations—idols that had to be removed in order for me to fully reconnect with God. I am so thankful that God empowered me to remove those idols from my life and saved me from my distractions.

I can't overemphasize the importance of removing all the distractions from your life—anything that is competing for your attention and keeping you from hearing God through his Word. If you're so distracted that you can't even find time to read the Bible and pray on a daily basis, then that is where you must begin. I know that sounds pretty basic, but that is where so many Christians start to go off track—when they neglect the basics. It's what happened to me, and I've seen it happen with countless others, as well.

God's Word is such an important element of our relationship and communication with God—and it is freely available to us if we will just take the time. God's Word can change our hearts each and every day of our lives. No other book can correct, teach, rebuke, bless, inspire, encourage, and sustain us. God's Word really is alive. But like any living relationship, Scripture can't work if we don't do our part. Meditating on it and applying it to our daily circumstances take deliberate intention, discipline, and action. Thankfully, God gives us the power to do this through the work of the Holy Spirit.

Imagine that God is sitting across the table from you as you read your Bible. He's there, you know, even though you can't see him. Take a minute to read a passage of Scripture while visualizing

God's presence with you. He wants to speak to you through his Word. He wants you to tell him all about your day, and he has advice to give you about how to go about the plans you've made. Read Scripture *with* him, and listen to what he says. Tell him your thoughts about what you are reading, and allow his wisdom to penetrate your heart.

Colossians 3:1-17 has deeply affected me since the renewal of my relationship with God. As an example of how much can be found in even a small portion of God's Word, I want to take time to unpack the verses for you. This passage means a lot to me personally and has greatly affected my relationship with God. It's like a summary of the New Testament for me. I have decided to meditate on Colossians 3 every day of my life from now on. Each day I approach it differently. I review the verses in my mind, reflecting on what it means to live out these godly principles. I want to be a walking letter that communicates the truth of Colossians 3 to everyone who knows me. Let me share with you what God has revealed to me as he has brought these words to life, and let me invite you to meditate on these verses for the next ten days.

DAY 1: "Set your hearts on things above."

"Since, then, you have been raised with Christ, set your hearts on things above, where Christ is seated at the right hand of God." COLOSSIANS 3:1

What this verse has impressed on my heart is that Christ has lifted me up, *away* from something. He has raised me up from something low. I envision him lifting me above the things of this world. He has removed me beyond the gravitational pull of worldly things. He has separated me from addiction to the things of this world. He has lifted me away from my negative emotions. He has lifted me up, away from the expectations of this world, away from the affections of this world.

After my three near-death experiences, the fact that my physical body will one day occupy a grave became very real to me. The truth is, no one knows when his or her time will come. But now I can read this verse with a new hope that death cannot keep me from the love of God. He has lifted me up, out of my sin, out of my spiritual grave. As you read this verse, picture your own grave or tombstone and think about how low, how deep, death can take you. Then imagine Christ lifting you out of your grave by the power of his love and grace, lifting you up to a place of honor beside him. There is no better place to be.

"Since you have been raised to new life with Christ, set your sights on the realities of heaven, where Christ sits in the place of honor at God's right hand."[1] Meditating on the "realities of heaven," the reality of my "new life with Christ," makes me want to set my heart on the things that are above, the things that are valuable to Christ, the things that are a priority to him, and the things that are important to his kingdom. What is important to Christ is now also important to me.

I also like how the 1937 Charles Williams translation of Colossians 3:1 emphasizes that we are to "keep on seeking the things above." It's a lifelong, continual process.

When I read this verse, I visualize myself alongside Jesus, lifted high away from the pull of this world, where I am free from my sin. Jesus is God's right-hand man, with all the power and authority to be my mediator. I picture Jesus with a scepter in his hand, crushing his enemies under his feet. I, too, am privileged to fight for God's truth, and through his power I can overcome the enemy's schemes and say no to my lower nature. As I seek the things that are important to Christ, I have joined in his divine fellowship with God, which transcends this world. I picture myself seated with Christ at the right hand of my heavenly Father.

DAY 2: "Set your minds on things above."

"Set your minds on things above, not on earthly things."

COLOSSIANS 3:2

L

When God got my attention at the Marriott Hotel, the verse that came to mind was Colossians 3:2. Verse 1 tells us to set our *hearts* on things above, and verse 2 now emphasizes our *minds*. What's the difference? Obviously, there is an intimate connection between the heart and the mind. Setting the mind on things above means that God governs our thought life and our will. In other words, everything I think about and everything I decide to do is viewed from God's perspective, against the backdrop of eternity.

I don't want to set my heart (my desires and affections) and my mind (my thoughts and decisions) on the things of the earth. Earthly things are not all evil; not everything pulls us away from God. But some of the things of this world that compete with our relationship with God include wealth, power, fame, and other pleasures. To make these things goals of my life is wrong. When I am raised with Christ, my life goals become radically different.

I like what *The Living Bible* says in verse 2: "Let heaven fill your thoughts; don't spend your time worrying about things down here."

Meditating on the first two verses of Colossians 3 is what really changed my life. I stopped expecting to be satisfied by anything from this earth. I stopped wanting anything other than Christ to give my life meaning. I set my heart's desires on him and fixed my mind on everything that is important to him. My earthly expectations changed to godly expectations. I now expect Christ alone to give me life and grace. I expect Christ alone to give me love, joy, peace, patience, kindness, goodness, faithfulness, gentleness, and self-control. I expect Christ alone to bring out all the fruit of the Spirit in me.[2] I can even trust him for miracles and healing. My only expectation now is that God will meet all my needs.[3]

My relationships with others have been renewed as God has changed my heart through the truths of Colossians 3. I'm no longer stuck on earthly things, thinking only about myself. God has given me a heart for other people. At the height of my celebrity, I tried to avoid people. I didn't want to be bothered, and I didn't care all that much about the things that people would say to me. I was aloof and often irritable. Today, I'm much more open to other people, and I have once again become approachable. I don't hold my unrealistic expectations over people's heads like I once did. I'm much more willing to accept the fact that we all make mistakes, and I realize that effective communication takes effort and persistence.

Relationships are hard work, but they're worth it because of their eternal value. It's pretty hard to hurt my feelings anymore, but when someone does, I handle it quite differently than I used to. I try not to take it personally, and I work toward understanding. Before, I would get angry and complain about the other person's flaws, instead of actively participating in the process of reconciliation. Grabbing hold of the apostle Paul's words in Colossians 3 has changed my life. It has caused me to have a quieter spirit.

Day 3: "Your life is now hidden with Christ."

"For you died, and your life is now hidden with Christ in God." COLOSSIANS 3:3

After three brushes with death in a short span of time, I gained a deeper understanding of Paul's message. I died, but I'm still alive, and my life is now hidden with Christ. You might read this same verse and think, *What do I have to die to?* Each of us must ask God this question. I had to die to the things of this earth—everything I thought I could gain, or had gained. I had to die by giving up my expectations. I had to die to myself, my agenda, and my goals. What do *you* have to die to?

As Christians, we have chosen to enter into union with Christ in his death and resurrection. This means that whatever is alien to Christ is now alien to us. Being hidden with God means that our lives now belong to a very real, yet invisible, realm. We are hidden with Christ in God, where our lives are safe and secure.

As I meditated further on this verse, I began to visualize Christ taking hold of my hand and walking together with me into the arms of God, who holds us both. I am now sitting with Jesus at the right hand of God the Father. God is protecting me, caring for me, and loving me. I have a sense of overwhelming peace as I am protected by my loving Father. My connection with Christ and God is a reality that I can experience *now*, not just later when I get to heaven. This realization was a watershed moment in my walk with God.

DAY 4: "Christ . . . is your life."

"When Christ, who is your life, appears, then you also
will appear with him in glory."   COLOSSIANS 3:4

To better understand this verse, I found it helpful to put myself *in*
the scene by personalizing the wording: "When Christ, who is now
my life, is revealed to the world, I also will be revealed with him in all
his glory." My life is now hidden with Christ, and Christ is also my
future hope. He alone gives me life and nurtures it. This verse reminds me of the future revelation of Christ's presence that we await.
I like to picture Christ returning to earth as he has promised us he
will, yet I can't fully imagine how glorious that day will be. Scripture gives us some idea: "I saw heaven standing open and there before me was a white horse, whose rider is called Faithful and
True. . . . On his robe and on his thigh he has this name written:
KING OF KINGS AND LORD OF LORDS."[4] Trumpets will blast, the
sky will burst forth with the joy of God's Son, and everyone will
bow at his name. On that day the world will also be dazzled by
Christ's unspeakable glory, and no one will be able to escape it. The
whole world will finally know that he is indeed Lord.

Though we're surrounded by many false gods, all vying for our
attention and our allegiance, this verse gives me great hope that one
day everything will be reconciled to Christ's lordship. We can hope
in his complete and future reign, when there will be no more decep-
tion, no more crying, and no more pain. All will be well. But in the
meantime—right here, right now—while our lives are hidden with
Christ in God, awaiting his triumphant return, we can devote our
lives to promoting God's glory.

I had read this passage many times before my renewal

experience, but it hadn't penetrated my heart in quite the same way. Just reading the Bible wasn't enough. I had to come to a place of really wanting to know God and hear what he had to say. I had to come to a place of being willing to sacrifice my own glory in favor of God's glory. For years, my worldly idols prevented me from growing further in my relationship with God. I was caught up in my own "stuff," my own glory, even though I would have told you at the time that I was doing it all for Christ. It sounds so simple to "glorify God," but it can be so difficult to let go of the things that we use to pacify ourselves, the things that distract us from glorifying God. There is so much to gain if we are willing to give it all up for God. Once I determined in my heart to give up my idols, God's grace was right there to bless my decision and empower my will to choose God above all else.

DAY 5: "Put to death . . . whatever belongs to your earthly nature."

"Put to death, therefore, whatever belongs to your earthly nature: sexual immorality, impurity, lust, evil desires and greed, which is idolatry. Because of these, the wrath of God is coming. You used to walk in these ways, in the life you once lived. But now you must rid yourselves of all such things as these: anger, rage, malice, slander, and filthy language from your lips." COLOSSIANS 3:5-8

The Living Bible added some perspective to my understanding of these verses: "Deaden the evil desires lurking within you; . . . don't worship the good things of life, for that is idolatry. . . . Now is the time to cast off and throw away all these rotten garments of anger, hatred, cursing, and dirty language."[5] What are we to cast off and throw away? Immorality in all its forms. We're to put these things "to death." These are *actions* that *we* take to break free of sin in all of its earthly forms, but God's power within us makes this possible. Think about it: We have the unfathomable, unlimited power of God within us, enabling us to break free from sexual temptations, greed, and anger; we can control our thoughts and our imaginations through his power. Not on our own, but through the power of God, all things are possible.[6]

When I first grasped the power of these verses and began to put to death my own earthly nature, I visualized a huge, raging fire into which I began to throw the things I was struggling with. I pictured myself throwing in each sin, calling it by name. The fire grew in intensity as the flames burned away my sins, leaving behind puffs of smoke and ashes. I have repeated this visualization many times as God has revealed my sinful thoughts, actions, and tendencies.

Like every man, I have struggled with sexual temptations. I have never given in to fornication or adultery, but too often in my life I have allowed sexually impure thoughts to take hold in my mind. I know the temptation of lust. But now, because of Christ's work in me, I have died to my desire for such pleasure, and I am almost completely free from my old nature in this regard. Instead of merely suppressing my sinful desires, I can actually wipe them out! Christ has lifted me away from the pressures of our sexually motivated culture, and there have been months when I don't even think about such things. (Of course, there are also moments when the temptation seems overwhelming, but that's why it's a daily battle, and that's why victory is an ongoing process.) It has been a joy to watch Christ heal me, renew my mind, and save me from old thought patterns. I've never met anyone who is completely free from temptation, every day, all the time, but I have seen substantial victory in my own life and in the lives of others. We're all works in progress, but I have seen firsthand that the power of God is real.

The next sin mentioned in Colossians 3:5 is *impurity*, which is anything unclean or unholy. Our natural tendency when we're tempted to be impure is to hide from God in shame, as Adam and Eve did after the Fall. But if we remember that as Christians we are hidden *with* Christ, not hidden *from* him, it changes our whole perspective on temptation. To remain hidden with Christ, we can't participate in anything immoral. So, when we're tempted to sin, we need to remember *where we are*—hidden with Christ in God! Of course, we could never remain pure on our own. We must avail ourselves of the power of the Holy Spirit within us to keep us clean.

The third sin listed here is *lust*, which is any *passion* for ungodly things. Lust actually means an uncontrolled desire. Have you ever felt as if your desires were controlling you? Maybe you have been battling an addiction of some sort. A lust for food can control what you do each day. Or perhaps you feel as if you don't have control over your anger. We must surrender to Christ any impulse we have that is out of control. That includes any desire that rules us instead of Christ ruling us.[7] Paul tells us not to gratify the desires of our sinful nature.[8] If I am expecting to find a life of fulfillment according to the world's standards, I can't expect life from God at the same time. As the apostle John warns us, "Do not love the world or the things in the world."[9]

Throughout my life, and particularly during the years leading up to my kidney transplant, I struggled with these sins mentioned in Colossians 3. I succumbed to the desire to have more of everything all the time—more money, more possessions, a bigger house, a nicer car, a secure future. I wanted my reputation to be such that people would recognize me and say, "Now there is one successful man." Driven by greed and impurity, I was given to anger and malice when I didn't get my way.

Now I recognize that everything I have, and all wisdom and knowledge, comes from God. All my possessions and success are fleeting, with no eternal value in God's economy. I knew that, but it had slipped from my heart. Now I want God's passions to be my passions—not passions for the things of this world, but passions for heavenly things, things that will last for eternity.

Can you imagine that God will set you free as you meditate on these few verses? God's truth has truly set me free, and he can do the same thing for you as you read the Bible and allow the Word of God to come alive in your heart and mind.

Not only did God set me free from such sins, he also changed my emotions. I really struggled with anger for that dark decade of my life. I am now much slower to anger, and I don't have frequent outbursts of anger. For years, I lived with toxic levels of anger built up inside me. I was constantly upset with my family, my ministry partners, my friends, my constituents and supporters, my editors, my publishers. You name it, I was upset about it.

Because of God's Spirit in me, I am overcoming my anger. He has freed me from indignation and the desire for revenge. He is continually freeing me from malice, which is a depravity of wickedness and ill will toward others. I mentioned earlier in my story that I felt surrounded by incompetence. I failed to see the worth of other people and thought they were bothersome. I wrongly viewed my relationships and made rash and ignorant judgments about people. I thought too highly of myself. But God has been freeing me from this general attitude of hostility and irritation toward other people.

God is also freeing me from making slanderous statements, pronouncing defaming judgments, criticizing and judging people for their behavior. This is precisely what Jesus warns against: "Do not judge, or you too will be judged. For in the same way you judge others, you will be judged, and with the measure you use, it will be measured to you."[10] When we judge others, it's no wonder God will judge us, because we are guilty of the same things.

DAY 6: "You have . . . put on the new self."

"Stop lying to one another, for you have stripped off the old self with its practices, and have put on the new self which is in the process of being made new in the likeness of its Creator, so that you may attain a perfect knowledge of Him. In this new relation there is no Greek and Jew, no circumcised and uncircumcised, no barbarian, Scythian, slave and freeman, but Christ is everything and in us all."

COLOSSIANS 3:9-11, WNT

I love the way the Williams translation of the New Testament emphasizes the fact that we are "in the process of being made new in the likeness of [our] Creator." As we are hidden with Christ in God, we *strip off* the old self—those "rotten garments" of anger, hatred, and so on—and we *put on* the new self. It's a process, and one that gradually, steadily, inevitably makes us new in the likeness—the image—of God our Creator. When we put on the new self, we are no longer concerned about our differences with one another. We are only concerned about our resemblance to Christ, who is *everything.*

DAY 7: "Clothe yourselves with compassion."

"Therefore, as God's chosen people, holy and dearly loved, clothe yourselves with compassion, kindness, humility, gentleness and patience." COLOSSIANS 3:12

When we strip off the rotten garments of our old sinful nature, we're not left standing naked in the public square. Instead, we're instructed to clothe ourselves with compassion, kindness, humility, gentleness, and patience.

Compassion enables us to feel the burdens of others, just as Christ feels our burdens. If we will take time to listen to God, he will faithfully show us how to extend compassion to other people in our lives. Each morning, I think about the people I will see in the course of my day. I want to have a heart of compassion for each one. By making this a matter of prayer, I find that my heart is more tender and sensitive to them when we meet.

Next, God wants us to be clothed in humility. This is something that Christ imparts to us as a result of our being lifted up with him. He is the supreme example of humility. He emptied himself of all authority and took on human flesh so that he could walk among us (Philippians 2). Because of his love for us, Christ stooped to our level and denied himself of what was rightfully his. He put himself at the bottom of the list and emptied himself of all status.

Humbling myself isn't always easy to do, but I think of it this way: If I'm with five other people, taking on the humility of Christ means that I consider myself to be sixth in level of importance. I realize that there is no real distinction between myself and other people, but I show them preference out of respect for Jesus Christ, who modeled this behavior for us. Learning to follow Christ's example has helped me put myself in proper perspective.

The other night, I went out with some friends for dinner, and as we were seated, I sensed the Holy Spirit say to me, "Let them order their meal first." It was such a simple thing, but I'm not naturally the sort of person to think about extending such grace when my stomach is growling. It was a small gesture, and I don't take credit for it because I know that God has done a work in me, and he continues to work on making me completely new.

Verse 12 also tells us to clothe ourselves with patience. I mentioned at the outset of the book that patience has never been one of my strengths. For me, waiting and having the ability to endure unfavorable situations are some of the most difficult tests of all. Clothing myself with patience means that I have to be steadfast, not anxious or worried. Looking at my natural inclinations, it seems I can always wait to give, but I have a harder time waiting to receive. My desire, however, is to be just the opposite of that. I want to wait patiently on the Lord every day for him to renew me. I want to pray and listen for his response, even when it doesn't come right away. I want to be careful to keep my relationship with God centered on what his Word says so that I may exude the patience of Christ to other people. And I want to give freely of myself to others.

DAY 8: "Forgive whatever grievances you may have."

"Bear with each other and forgive whatever grievances you may have against one another. Forgive as the Lord forgave you." COLOSSIANS 3:13

Hand in hand with *patience* goes the need to "bear with each other." We are called to be faithful friends and members of the body of Christ. Sometimes we want to give up on each other, but God tells us to persevere. In our society, Christians are often depicted as narrow-minded and unforgiving. I want to break this stereotype, no matter how different someone is from me. I look around at the youth culture today and find myself feeling very detached from the body-piercing, tattoo-wearing teenagers. Nevertheless, I know that they, too, are created in God's image and are precious to him. I don't want to be egocentric, holding to a view that my education, upbringing, and life experience are "right." I want to value my life experience but never fail to see the value of other life experiences. I don't want to judge other people but want to listen and be curious and fascinated by their uniqueness. I want to learn from them.

As we bear with one another, we're also told to "forgive whatever grievances [we] may have against one another," and forgive as the Lord has forgiven us—which is to say, freely. I want to forgive every offense done against me and receive forgiveness from everyone I have offended. I want to be generous in extending grace. I want to erase any grudges that are written on my heart. I want to set people free.

The Greek word for *forgiveness* has two root meanings. One is "to pardon or set someone free; to release." The other is "to untie chains or ropes that bind something." In other words, we must understand that the people who wound us and offend us are people who have been wounded and offended themselves. When we forgive them, we untie the ropes of pain and resentment that bind them, and we are set free as well.

DAY 9: "Over all these virtues put on love."

"And over all these virtues put on love, which binds them all together in perfect unity." COLOSSIANS 3:14

As we set people free through the power of forgiveness, we are bound up together with them in perfect unity, through the power of love. Love is the ribbon that ties all the virtues together. Love is the one debt we can never pay off.[11] When we love our neighbor as we love ourselves, we fulfill all the requirements of the law.[12] Paul tells us that love is one of three virtues that will remain—along with faith and hope—so we had better get this one right![13] First Corinthians 13 can really help us understand what it means to bear with one another and put on love.

Perhaps you find yourself wondering how you can clothe yourself with all that these verses suggest. That's where grace comes in. Grace is God's power, given to us so that we can live lives that are pleasing to him. God gives grace to the humble, but he opposes people who are prideful.[14]

DAY 10: "Let the peace of Christ rule in your hearts."

"Let the peace of Christ rule in your hearts, since as members of one body you were called to peace. And be thankful." COLOSSIANS 3:15

Verse 15 is one of my favorite verses in Colossians 3. As I have learned to surrender my hopes and dreams and plans and purposes to Christ and to submit to his direction for my life, I have found that his peace has come to rule in my heart. Whereas, before, my life was in almost constant turmoil—and everyone around me knew it!—today I can say that I am much more at peace with myself, with God, and with other people. My life is still not perfect in this regard, but it is so much better than it was.

"Let the word of Christ dwell in you richly as you teach and admonish one another with all wisdom, and as you sing psalms, hymns and spiritual songs with gratitude in your hearts to God" (v. 16). Scripture reminds me that I have the word of Christ—his truth—dwelling within me. Because of that, I can teach and admonish others, according to God's wisdom, and sing with gratitude in my heart to God.

As you meditate on this verse, imagine that God is touching every part of you, from head to toe. Picture yourself overflowing with the wisdom he has given you through his Word. When you wake up in the morning, imagine what you will say to the people you meet during the day that will express God's love. Throughout your day, with each person you encounter, share your heart of gratitude toward God. If that doesn't turn your world around, nothing will!

"Whatever you do, whether in word or deed, do it all in the name of the Lord Jesus, giving thanks to God the Father through him" (v. 17). I want everything I say and everything I do to be centered in Christ. I want to start every day by reminding myself of all the acts of God's loving-kindness in my life. For many years, I did not live in the fullness of the truth of Colossians 3. Now, I find that it challenges me every day, and I am continually changing as I yield to what the Spirit says to me. And just as the Word of God has changed me, it can change you.

As you meditate on this passage of Scripture, picture yourself seated on a throne. Out loud, ask Christ to be the center of your life. As you do, stand up and step down from the throne, relinquishing control of your life to Christ the King. Sit down on the floor beside the throne and wait for Christ to direct you by his wisdom and his Word.

Ask the Lord to show you fresh ways to look at his Word. He will give you insights, images, and impressions that will bring his truth to light and to life. Take time to meditate on Scripture and listen for the voice of the Lord to speak to you. You will find that Christ is faithful to renew your heart, mind, and soul.

YOUR RELATIONSHIP WITH GOD

1. After reading these meditations, in what ways have you determined to "set your heart on things above"?

2. What are some guidelines for holy living found in Colossians 3:1-17 that can help you grow in your relationship with God?

3. Are you living out of a heart of gratitude? What happens to your relationship with God when you are not thankful? Read Ezekiel 36:26 and ask God to give you a "heart of flesh."

KEY VERSES: Memorize Colossians 3:1-17, or choose your own passage of Scripture and memorize it. (I'm telling you, it will change your life!)

MAKING IT PERSONAL

Write out the passage you chose to memorize and explain what it means to you. How does it affect your relationship with God? What do you feel God wants to teach you right now from these verses? Make a habit of reviewing these verses daily.

APPENDIX
NAMES AND ATTRIBUTES OF GOD

Advocate (1 John 2:1, NKJV)
Almighty (Revelation 1:8; Matthew 28:18)
Alpha and Omega (Revelation 1:8; 22:13, NKJV)
Atoning Sacrifice for Our Sins (1 John 2:2)
Author and Perfecter of our Faith (Hebrews 12:2)
Author of Life (Acts 3:15)
Author of Salvation (Hebrews 2:10)
Beginning and End (Revelation 22:13)
Blessed and Only Ruler (1 Timothy 6:15)
Bread of Life (John 6:35, 48)
Capstone (Acts 4:11; 1 Peter 2:7)
Chief Cornerstone (Ephesians 2:20)
Chief Shepherd (1 Peter 5:4)
Christ (1 John 2:22)
Creator (John 1:3)
Deliverer (Romans 11:26)
Eternal Life (1 John 1:2; 5:20)
Everlasting Father (Isaiah 9:6)
Gate (John 10:9)
Faithful and True (Revelation 19:11)
Faithful and True Witness (Revelation 3:14)
Faithful Witness (Revelation 1:5)
First and Last (Revelation 1:17; 2:8; 22:13)
Firstborn from the Dead (Revelation 1:5)
God (John 1:1; 20:28; Romans 9:5; Hebrews 1:8; 2 Peter 1:1; 1 John 5:20)
Good Shepherd (John 10:11, 14)
Great High Priest (Hebrews 4:14)
Great Shepherd (Hebrews 13:20)
Head of the Church (Ephesians 1:22; 4:15; 5:23)
Heir of All Things (Hebrews 1:2)
High Priest (Hebrews 2:17)
Holy and True (Revelation 3:7)
Holy One (Acts 3:14)
Hope (1 Timothy 1:1)
Hope of Glory (Colossians 1:27)
Horn of Salvation (Luke 1:69)

I AM (John 8:58)
Image of God (2 Corinthians 4:4)
King Eternal (1 Timothy 1:17)
King of Israel (John 1:49)
King of Kings (1 Timothy 6:15; Revelation 19:16)
King of the Ages (Revelation 15:3)
King of the Jews (Matthew 27:11)
Lamb (Revelation 13:8)
Lamb of God (John 1:29)
Lamb without Blemish (1 Peter 1:19)
Last Adam (1 Corinthians 15:45)
Life (John 14:6; Colossians 3:4)
Light of the World (John 8:12)
Lion of the Tribe of Judah (Revelation 5:5)
Living One (Revelation 1:18)
Living Stone (1 Peter 2:4)
Lord (2 Peter 2:20)
Lord of All (Acts 10:36)
Lord of Glory (1 Corinthians 2:8)
Lord of Lords (Revelation 19:16)
LORD [YHWH] our Righteousness (Jeremiah 23:6)
Man from Heaven (1 Corinthians 15:48)
Mediator of the New Covenant (Hebrews 9:15)
Mighty God (Isaiah 9:6)
Morning Star (Revelation 22:16)
Offspring of David (Revelation 22:16)
Only Begotten Son of God (John 1:18, NKJV; 1 John 4:9, NKJV)
Our Great God and Savior (Titus 2:13)
Our Holiness (1 Corinthians 1:30)
Our Husband (2 Corinthians 11:2)
Our Protection (2 Thessalonians 3:3)
Our Redemption (1 Corinthians 1:30)
Our Righteousness (1 Corinthians 1:30)
Our Sacrificed Passover Lamb (1 Corinthians 5:7)
Power of God (1 Corinthians 1:24)
Precious Cornerstone (1 Peter 2:6)
Prince of Peace (Isaiah 9:6)
Prophet (Acts 3:22)
Resurrection and Life (John 11:25)
Righteous Branch (Jeremiah 23:5)
Righteous One (Acts 7:52; 1 John 2:1)
Rock (1 Corinthians 10:4)
Root of David (Revelation 5:5; 22:16)
Ruler of God's Creation (Revelation 3:14)

Ruler of the Kings of the Earth (Revelation 1:5)
Savior (Ephesians 5:23; Titus 1:4; 3:6; 2 Peter 2:20)
Son of David (Luke 18:39)
Son of God (John 1:49; Hebrews 4:14)
Son of Man (Matthew 8:20)
Son of the Most High God (Luke 1:32)
Source of Eternal Salvation for All Who Obey Him (Hebrews 5:9)
The One Mediator (1 Timothy 2:5)
The Stone That the Builders Rejected (Acts 4:11)
True Bread (John 6:32)
True Light (John 1:9)
True Vine (John 15:1)
Truth (John 1:14; 14:6)
Way (John 14:6)
Wisdom of God (1 Corinthians 1:24)
Wonderful Counselor (Isaiah 9:6)
Word of God (Revelation 19:13)
Word of Life (1 John 1:1)

NOTES

CHAPTER 1
1. Mark 8:36

CHAPTER 2
1. 1 Peter 2:2

CHAPTER 3
1. Philippians 4:19
2. Luke 22:42
3. Luke 22:44
4. Gerald G. May, *Addiction and Grace* (San Francisco: Harper & Row, 1988).

CHAPTER 4
1. 2 Corinthians 10:5
2. Ephesians 5:15-16
3. John 10:10
4. Ephesians 3:16-21
5. James 4:6-8
6. James 1:19-20
7. Ephesians 4:29
8. Proverbs 4:23
9. Proverbs 3:5-6
10. See Galatians 5:22-23.
11. Galatians 5:25
12. Colossians 3:3
13. See Daniel 7:14.
14. 2 Timothy 1:7, NKJV
15. See John 8:32.
16. Colossians 3:2
17. Job 31:1
18. See Proverbs 4:23, NASB.

CHAPTER 5
1. See Philippians 1:6.
2. Mark 12:30-31
3. See Matthew 22:36-40.
4. The 5 *M*'s are adapted from my book *Joy That Lasts* (Grand Rapids: Zondervan, revised edition, 2000). A more complete discussion of the 5 *M*'s can be found there.

5. See Ephesians 2:10.
6. 1 Thessalonians 5:18
7. James 1:2-4
8. See Matthew 5:45, NKJV.
9. See Job 1:6-12.
10. Job 42:1-3

CHAPTER 6

1. M. Scott Peck, *The Road Less Traveled*, second Touchstone edition (New York: Touchstone, 1998), 15.
2. Luke 21:17, 19
3. Philippians 4:19
4. Hebrews 5:8-9
5. James 1:4
6. 1 Thessalonians 5:18

CHAPTER 7

1. See Matthew 6:25-34; 10:29-31; Luke 12:6-7, 27-31.
2. James 1:5
3. James 3:17
4. Don Colbert, *Deadly Emotions: Understand the Mind-Body-Spirit Connection That Can Heal or Destroy You* (Nashville: Nelson, 2003), 140–142.
5. Ibid., 141–142.
6. Linda Song, Gary Schwartz, and Linda Russek, "Heart-Focused Attention and Heart-Brain Synchronization: Energetic and Physiological Mechanisms," in *Alternative Therapies in Health and Medicine*, 1998, volume 4, number 5, 44–62.
7. Proverbs 4:23
8. Philippians 4:13, NKJV
9. See Proverbs 3:5-6.
10. James 1:19

CHAPTER 8

1. Luke 22:42
2. Emilie Griffin, *Clinging: The Experience of Prayer* (New York: McCracken, 1994), 13.
3. James 4:8
4. Romans 12:2
5. William Law, *The Spirit of Prayer* (1749), part 1, chapter 2, prayer 1.2–23; see online at www.spiritofprayer.com/wlaw02.php for the text of this book.
6. Romans 5:1-2, NRSV
7. Watchman Nee, *The Normal Christian Life*, American edition (Wheaton, Ill.: Tyndale, 1977), 143.
8. Calvin Miller, *Into the Depths of God* (Minneapolis: Bethany, 2000).

9. Galatians 2:20, NKJV
10. 1 Peter 1:6-7
11. 1 Timothy 4:7-8
12. Philippians 3:12

MEDITATIONS ON COLOSSIANS 3

1. Colossians 3:1, NLT
2. See Galatians 5:22-23.
3. See Philippians 4:19.
4. Revelation 19:11, 16
5. Colossians 3:5, 8, TLB
6. See Matthew 19:26; Philippians 4:13.
7. See 1 Peter 1:14-15.
8. See Galatians 5:16.
9. 1 John 2:15, NKJV
10. Matthew 7:1-2
11. See Romans 13:8.
12. See Romans 13:9-10.
13. See 1 Corinthians 13:13.
14. See Proverbs 3:34; James 4:6.

ABOUT THE AUTHOR

Dr. Gary Smalley, the cofounder and chairman of the board of Smalley Relationship Center, is America's relationship doctor. He is the author or coauthor of more than forty books, including the best-selling, award-winning books *Marriage for a Lifetime, Secrets to Lasting Love,* and *The Blessing.* Releases within the past several years include the best-selling *The DNA of Relationships, Men's Relational Toolbox, Food and Love, Bound by Honor,* and the Redemption fiction series, coauthored with Karen Kingsbury.

In addition to earning a master's degree from Bethel Theological Seminary, Gary has received two honorary doctorates, one from Biola University, and one from Southwest Baptist University, for his work with couples.

In his thirty years of ministry, Gary has appeared on national television programs such as *Oprah, Larry King Live,* and *Today,* as well as numerous national radio programs. Gary has produced films and videos that have sold millions of copies. Gary and his wife, Norma, have been married for forty-two years and live in Branson, Missouri. They have three adult children and eight grandchildren.

THE DNA OF RELATIONSHIPS
BY DR. GARY SMALLEY

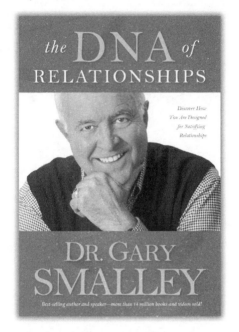

Repeating the Same Mistakes in Your Relationships?

DR. GARY SMALLEY TELLS YOU
THE WHYS AND HOWS OF RELATIONSHIPS:

· Discover the fear dance that occurs in all relationships.

· Explore how to create safety in relationships.

· Cultivate healthy habits that care for your emotional needs.

· Find out how to listen to other people's emotions.

CP0166

LOOK FOR THESE ADDITIONAL RELATIONSHIP RESOURCES WHEREVER FINE BOOKS ARE SOLD:

YOUR RELATIONSHIP WITH GOD
by Dr. Gary Smalley

God is trying to get your attention. Are you listening? At the height of his success as a popular counselor, author, and speaker, Gary found himself frustrated, disappointed, and worn out. Sound familiar? In *Your Relationship with God*, Gary Smalley writes about how God gave him a wake-up call he could never forget. His life, his heart, and his outlook on life were changed forever. Gary wants you to experience that same life change. Discover today how you can recognize God's voice in your life.

MEN'S RELATIONAL TOOLBOX
by Dr. Gary Smalley, Dr. Greg Smalley, and Michael Smalley

Men understand the world in a unique way—and they approach relationships in a special way as well. This book is designed to help guys figure out the nuts and bolts of satisfying relationships—both at work and at home.

THE DNA OF RELATIONSHIPS FOR COUPLES
by Dr. Greg Smalley and Dr. Robert Paul

Through the stories of four fictionalized couples, Greg Smalley and Robert Paul help readers understand how to work at correcting dangerous relationship habits. The lives of the couples depicted in the book illustrate how to break the fear dance, create safety in a relationship, listen to each other's emotions, and much more. This book is a unique relationship book that uses stories to demonstrate what real relationship change looks like.

THE MARRIAGE YOU'VE ALWAYS DREAMED OF
by Dr. Greg Smalley

Discover what the marriage you've always dreamed of looks like. Find out how to transform marriage problems into opportunities to love each other—how to look for treasures in the trials. Discover how to experience God's best for your marriage.

DON'T DATE NAKED
by Michael and Amy Smalley

Straight talk to single guys and girls on what healthy relationships look like.

THE
SMALLEY RELATIONSHIP
CENTER

The Smalley Relationship Center, founded by Gary and Norma Smalley, offers many varied resources and events to help people strengthen all their relationships. The center provides enrichment resources, conferences, small-group curricula, articles, and daily online encouragement. Resources include books, videos, DVDs, and small-group series for married couples, parents, and singles. Marriage seminars taught by Dr. Gary Smalley, Dr. Greg Smalley, and Ted Cunningham are scheduled in cities throughout the United States.

Resources and Events:

- Videos series, including the classic, best-selling *Keys to Loving Relationships* and *Secrets to Lasting Love*

- Forty-five best-selling books, including *The DNA of Relationships* and the new *I Promise* marriage book

- Small-group resources, including *The DNA of Relationships, Homes of Honor,* and the new *I Promise* marriage curriculum by Purpose Driven Ministries

- Online enrichment through more than four hundred articles, weekly e-letters, and weekly tips about relationships

- Live marriage seminars for churches

- Weekly free newsletter filled with practical articles on all your relationships

For more information on these resources or to inquire about live seminars, visit www.garysmalley.com or call (800) 84-TODAY (848-6329).